U.S. Department of Justice
Office of Justice Programs
National Institute of Justice

National Institute of Justice

Law Enforcement and Corrections Standards and Testing Program

**Ballistic Resistance of
Personal Body Armor**

NIJ Standard–0101.04

ABOUT THE LAW ENFORCEMENT AND CORRECTIONS STANDARDS AND TESTING PROGRAM

The Law Enforcement and Corrections Standards and Testing Program is sponsored by the Office of Science and Technology of the National Institute of Justice (NIJ), U.S. Department of Justice. The program responds to the mandate of the Justice System Improvement Act of 1979, which directed NIJ to encourage research and development to improve the criminal justice system and to disseminate the results to Federal, State, and local agencies.

The Law Enforcement and Corrections Standards and Testing Program is an applied research effort that determines the technological needs of justice system agencies, sets minimum performance standards for specific devices, tests commercially available equipment against those standards, and disseminates the standards and the test results to criminal justice agencies nationally and internationally.

The program operates through:

The *Law Enforcement and Corrections Technology Advisory Council* (LECTAC), consisting of nationally recognized criminal justice practitioners from Federal, State, and local agencies, which assesses technological needs and sets priorities for research programs and items to be evaluated and tested.

The *Office of Law Enforcement Standards* (OLES) at the National Institute of Standards and Technology, which develops voluntary national performance standards for compliance testing to ensure that individual items of equipment are suitable for use by criminal justice agencies. The standards are based upon laboratory testing and evaluation of representative samples of each item of equipment to determine the key attributes, develop test methods, and establish minimum performance requirements for each essential attribute. In addition to the highly technical standards, OLES also produces technical reports and user guidelines that explain in nontechnical terms the capabilities of available equipment.

The *National Law Enforcement and Corrections Technology Center (NLECTC),* operated by a grantee, which supervises a national compliance testing program conducted by independent laboratories. The standards developed by OLES serve as performance benchmarks against which commercial equipment is measured. The facilities, personnel, and testing capabilities of the independent laboratories are evaluated by OLES prior to testing each item of equipment, and OLES helps the NLECTC staff review and analyze data. Test results are published in Equipment Performance Reports designed to help justice system procurement officials make informed purchasing decisions.

Publications are available at no charge through the National Law Enforcement and Corrections Technology Center. Some documents are also available online through the Internet/World Wide Web. To request a document or additional information, call 800–248–2742 or 301–519–5060, or write:

National Law Enforcement and Corrections Technology Center
P.O. Box 1160
Rockville, MD 20849–1160
E-Mail: *asknlectc@nlectc.org*
World Wide Web address: *http://www.nlectc.org*

The National Institute of Justice is a component of the Office of Justice Programs, which also includes the Bureau of Justice Assistance, the Bureau of Justice Statistics, the Office of Juvenile Justice and Delinquency Prevention, and the Office for Victims of Crime.

U.S. Department of Justice
Office of Justice Programs
National Institute of Justice

Ballistic Resistance of Personal Body Armor

NIJ Standard–0101.04
*Supersedes NIJ Standard–0101.03, Ballistic Resistance
of Police Body Armor dated April 1987*

Coordination by:
Office of Law Enforcement Standards
National Institute of Standards and Technology
Gaithersburg, MD 20899–8102

Prepared for:
National Institute of Justice
Office of Science and Technology
Washington, DC 20531

September 2000

NCJ 183651

National Institute of Justice

Julie E. Samuels
Acting Director

The technical effort to develop this standard was conducted
under Interagency Agreement 94–IJ–R–004,
Project No. 98–001CTT.

This standard was formulated by the Office of Law Enforcement Standards (OLES)
of the National Institute of Standards and Technology (NIST),
Kathleen M. Higgins, Director. The participants in the research
and revision of this standard were: Carter K. Lord,
Former Test Coordinator and Ballistics Range Manager, OLES,
Steven L. Lightsey, President, The Tekne Group, Inc.,
Ken Malley, National Technical Systems (NTS), Fredricksburg, VA,
Nathaniel E. Waters, Engineering Technician, OLES,
and the Staff of National Technical Systems (NTS), Camden, AR.
The preparation of this standard was sponsored by the National Institute of Justice,
Dr. David G. Boyd, Director, Office of Science and Technology.

FOREWORD

This document, NIJ Standard–0101.04, "Ballistic Resistance of Personal Body Armor," is an equipment standard developed by the Office of Law Enforcement Standards (OLES) of the National Institute of Standards and Technology (NIST). It is produced as part of the Law Enforcement and Corrections Standards and Testing Program of the National Institute of Justice (NIJ).

This standard is a technical document that specifies the performance requirements that equipment should meet to satisfy the needs of criminal justice agencies for high quality service. While purchasers can use the test methods described in this standard to determine whether a particular piece of equipment meets the essential requirements, users are encouraged to have this testing conducted only in properly accredited laboratories. Procurement officials may also refer to this standard in their purchasing documents and require that equipment offered for purchase meet its requirements. Compliance with the requirements of this standard may be attested to by an independent laboratory or guaranteed by the vendor.

Because this standard is designed as a procurement aid, it provides precise and detailed test methods. For those who seek general guidance concerning the selection and application of law enforcement and corrections equipment, user guides have also been published. The guides explain in nontechnical language how to select equipment capable of the level of performance required by a purchasing agency.

NIJ STANDARD–0101.04 IS NOT INTENDED TO RESTRICT OR OTHERWISE INFLUENCE THE PROCUREMENT AND USE OF NIJ STANDARD–0101.03 COMPLIANT BODY ARMORS. THE PUBLICATION AND USE OF THIS REVISION FOR NEW MODEL COMPLIANCE TESTING DOES NOT INVALIDATE OR RENDER UNSUITABLE ANY BODY ARMOR MODELS PREVIOUSLY DETERMINED TO BE COMPLIANT USING NIJ STANDARD–0101.03 REQUIREMENTS.

NIJ standards are subjected to continuing research, development, testing, change, and review. This standard and its successors will be reevaluated annually for success in achieving the technical goals of this revision. These reviews will be based on data collected through the Compliance Testing Program and its certified test laboratories, as well as from valid comments from the user and manufacturing communities. Technical comments and recommended revisions are welcome. Please send all written comments and suggestions to the Director, Office of Science and Technology, National Institute of Justice, U.S. Department of Justice, 810 7th St., NW, Washington, DC 20531.

Before citing this or any other NIJ standard in a contract document, users should verify that the most recent edition of the standard is used. Write to the Director, Office of Law Enforcement Standards, National Institute of Standards and Technology, 100 Bureau Drive, Stop 8102, Gaithersburg, MD 20899–8102.

Dr. David G. Boyd, Director
Office of Science and Technology
National Institute of Justice

ACKNOWLEDGMENTS

This standard has been reviewed and approved by the Weapons and Protective Systems Subcommittee and the Executive Committee of the Law Enforcement and Corrections Technology Advisory Council (LECTAC) and also by the National Armor Advisory Board (NAAB), currently comprised of representatives from:

Accordis Fibers, Inc.
American Body Armor and Equipment Co.
California Department of Corrections
Chesterfield County Police Department, Virginia
Department of Justice
DHB Armor Group
DuPont Advanced Fiber Systems
Federal Bureau of Investigation
Fraternal Order of Police
Guardian Technologies, International
Hexcel Schwebel High Performance Fibers
Honeywell/Allied Signal, Inc.
International Association of Chiefs of Police
International Brotherhood of Police Officers
National Association of Police Organizations
National Sheriff's Association
Office of Community Oriented Policing Services
Protective Apparel Corporation of America
Safariland Ltd., Inc.
U.S. Armor Corporation
U.S. Secret Service, TSD/P&D

CONTENTS

TABLES

FIGURES

STANDARD SPECIFIC ABBREVIATIONS

ACP =	Automatic Colt Pistol		LR =	Long Rifle
ANSI =	American National Standards Institute		LRN =	Lead Round Nose
AP =	Armor Piercing		NLECTC =	National Law Enforcement and Corrections Technology Center
BFS =	Backface Signature			
BL =	Ballistic Limit		P-BFS =	Penetration and Backface Signature
BMF =	Backing Material Fixture		PP =	Partial Penetration
CP =	Complete Penetration		RN =	Round Nose
CPO =	Compliance Program Office		S&W =	Smith & Wesson
CTP =	Compliance Testing Program		SAAMI =	Sporting Arms and Ammunition Manufacturers Institute
CTR =	Compliance Test Report			
FMJ =	Full Metal Jacket		SJHP =	Semi Jacketed Hollow Point
JHP =	Jacketed Hollow Point		SJSP =	Semi Jacketed Soft Point
JSP =	Jacketed Soft Point			

COMMONLY USED SYMBOLS AND ABBREVIATIONS

A	ampere	H	henry	nm	nanometer
ac	alternating current	h	hour	No.	number
AM	amplitude modulation	hf	high frequency	o.d.	outside diameter
cd	candela	Hz	hertz	Ω	ohm
cm	centimeter	i.d.	inside diameter	p.	page
CP	chemically pure	in	inch	Pa	pascal
c/s	cycle per second	IR	infrared	pe	probable error
d	day	J	joule	pp.	pages
dB	decibel	L	lambert	ppm	parts per million
dc	direct current	L	liter	qt	quart
°C	degree Celsius	lb	pound	rad	radian
°F	degree Fahrenheit	lbf	pound-force	rf	radio frequency
diam	diameter	lbf·in	pound-force inch	rh	relative humidity
emf	electromotive force	lm	lumen	s	second
eq	equation	ln	logarithm (base e)	SD	standard deviation
F	farad	log	logarithm (base 10)	sec.	section
fc	footcandle	M	molar	SWR	standing wave ratio
fig.	figure	m	meter	uhf	ultrahigh frequency
FM	frequency modulation	min.	minute	UV	ultraviolet
ft	foot	mm	millimeter	V	volt
ft/s	foot per second	mph	miles per hour	vhf	very high frequency
g	acceleration	m/s	meter per second	W	watt
g	gram	N	newton	λ	wavelength
gr	grain	N·m	newton meter	wt	weight

area=unit^2 (e.g., ft^2, in^2, etc.); volume=unit^3 (e.g., ft^3, m^3, etc.)

PREFIXES

d	deci (10^{-1})	da	deka (10)
c	centi (10^{-2})	h	hecto (10^2)
m	milli (10^{-3})	k	kilo (10^3)
μ	micro (10^{-6})	M	mega (10^6)
n	nano (10^{-9})	G	giga (10^9)
p	pico (10^{-12})	T	tera (10^{12})

COMMON CONVERSIONS
(See ASTM E380)

0.30480 m = 1 ft	4.448222 N = 1 lbf
2.54 cm = 1 in	1.355818 J = 1 ft·lbf
0.4535924 kg = 1 lb	0.1129848 N m = 1 lbf·in
0.06479891g = 1 gr	14.59390 N/m = 1 lbf/ft
0.9463529 L = 1 qt	6894.757 Pa = 1 lbf/in^2
3600000 J = 1 kW·hr	1.609344 km/h = 1 mph

Temperature: $T_{°C} = (T_{°F}-32) \times 5/9$

Temperature: $T_{°F} = (T_{°C} \times 9/5) + 32$

NIJ STANDARD
FOR
BALLISTIC RESISTANCE OF PERSONAL BODY ARMOR

1. PURPOSE AND SCOPE

The purpose of this standard is to establish minimum performance requirements and test methods for the ballistic resistance of personal body armor intended to protect the torso against gunfire. This standard is a general revision of NIJ Standard–0101.03, dated April 1987, updating the labeling requirements, acceptance criteria, test ammunition, procedures, and other items throughout the standard.

The scope of the standard is limited to ballistic resistance only; this standard does not address threats from knives and sharply pointed instruments, which are different types of threat.

2. NIJ BODY ARMOR CLASSIFICATION

Personal body armors covered by this standard are classified into seven classes, or types, by level of ballistic performance. The ballistic threat posed by a bullet depends, among other things, on its composition, shape, caliber, mass, angle of incidence, and impact velocity. Because of the wide variety of bullets and cartridges available in a given caliber and because of the existence of handloaded ammunition, armors that will defeat a standard test round may not defeat other loadings in the same caliber. For example, an armor that prevents complete penetration by a 40 S&W test round may or may not defeat a 40 S&W round with higher velocity. In general, an armor that defeats a given lead bullet may not resist complete penetration by other bullets of the same caliber of different construction or configuration. The test ammunition specified in this standard represent general, common threats to law enforcement officers.

As of the year 2000, ballistic resistant body armor suitable for full time wear throughout an entire shift of duty is available in classification Types I, IIA, II, and IIIA, which provide increasing levels of protection from handgun threats. Type I body armor, which was first issued during the NIJ demonstration project in 1975, is the minimum level of protection that any officer should have. Officers seeking protection from lower velocity 9 mm and 40 S&W ammunition typically wear Type IIA body armor. For protection against high velocity 357 Magnum and higher velocity 9 mm ammunition, officers traditionally select Type II body armor. Type IIIA body armor provides the highest level of protection available in concealable body armor and provides protection from high velocity 9 mm and 44 Magnum ammunition.

Type IIIA armor is suitable for routine wear in many situations; however, departments located in hot, humid climates may need to carefully evaluate their use of Type IIIA body armor for their officers. Types III and IV armor, which protect against high powered rifle rounds, are clearly intended for use only in tactical situations when the threat warrants such protection (see app. C).

The classification of an armor panel that provides two or more levels of NIJ ballistic protection at different locations on the ballistic panel shall be that of the minimum ballistic protection provided at any location on the panel.

2.1   Type I (22 LR; 380 ACP)

This armor protects against .22 caliber Long Rifle Lead Round Nose (LR LRN) bullets, with nominal masses of 2.6 g (40 gr) impacting at a minimum velocity of 320 m/s (1050 ft/s) or less, and 380 ACP Full Metal Jacketed Round Nose (FMJ RN) bullets, with nominal masses of 6.2 g (95 gr) impacting at a minimum velocity of 312 m/s (1025 ft/s) or less.

2.2   Type IIA (9 mm; 40 S&W)

This armor protects against 9 mm Full Metal Jacketed Round Nose (FMJ RN) bullets, with nominal masses of 8.0 g (124 gr) impacting at a minimum velocity of 332 m/s (1090 ft/s) or less, and 40 S&W caliber Full Metal Jacketed (FMJ) bullets, with nominal masses of 11.7 g (180 gr) impacting at a minimum velocity of 312 m/s (1025 ft/s) or less. It also provides protection against the threats mentioned in section 2.1.

2.3   Type II (9 mm; 357 Magnum)

This armor protects against 9 mm Full Metal Jacketed Round Nose (FMJ RN) bullets, with nominal masses of 8.0 g (124 gr) impacting at a minimum velocity of 358 m/s (1175 ft/s) or less, and 357 Magnum Jacketed Soft Point (JSP) bullets, with nominal masses of 10.2 g (158 gr) impacting at a minimum velocity of 427 m/s (1400 ft/s) or less. It also provides protection against the threats mentioned in sections 2.1 and 2.2.

2.4   Type IIIA (High Velocity 9 mm; 44 Magnum)

This armor protects against 9 mm Full Metal Jacketed Round Nose (FMJ RN) bullets, with nominal masses of 8.0 g (124 gr) impacting at a minimum velocity of 427 m/s (1400 ft/s) or less, and 44 Magnum Jacketed Hollow Point (JHP) bullets, with nominal masses of 15.6 g (240 gr) impacting at a minimum velocity of 427 m/s (1400 ft/s) or less. It also provides protection against most handgun threats, as well as the threats mentioned in sections 2.1, 2.2, and 2.3.

2.5   Type III (Rifles)

This armor protects against 7.62 mm Full Metal Jacketed (FMJ) bullets (U.S. Military designation M80), with nominal masses of 9.6 g (148 gr) impacting at a minimum velocity of 838 m/s (2750 ft/s) or less. It also provides protection against the threats mentioned in sections 2.1, 2.2, 2.3, and 2.4.

2.6   Type IV (Armor Piercing Rifle)

This armor protects against .30 caliber armor piercing (AP) bullets (U.S. Military designation M2 AP), with nominal masses of 10.8 g (166 gr) impacting at a minimum velocity of 869 m/s (2850 ft/s) or less. It also provides at least single hit protection against the threats mentioned in sections 2.1, 2.2, 2.3, 2.4, and 2.5.

2.7   Special Type

A purchaser having a special requirement for a level of protection other than one of the above standard types and threat levels should specify the exact test round(s) and minimum reference impact velocities to be used, and indicate that this standard shall govern in all other aspects.

3. DEFINITIONS

3.1   Angle of Incidence

The angle between the line of flight of the bullet and the perpendicular to the front surface of the backing material fixture as shown in figure 1.

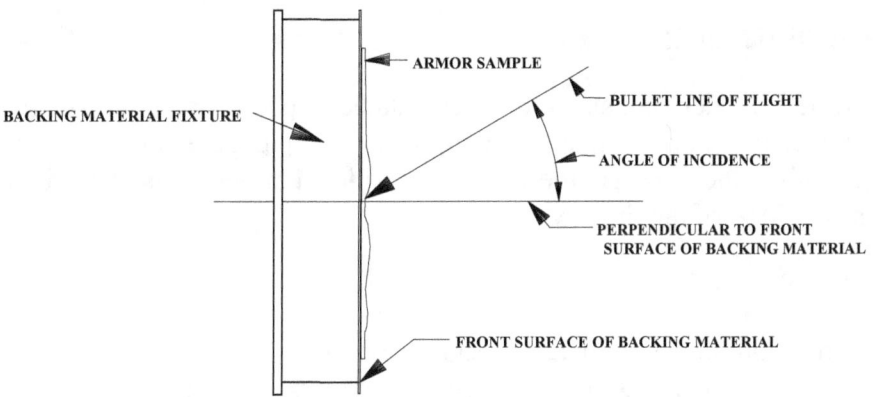

Figure 1. Angle of incidence

3.2   Armor Carrier

A component of the armor sample or armor panel whose primary purpose is to retain the ballistic panel and provide a means of supporting and securing the armor garment to the user. These carriers are not generally ballistic resistant.

3.3   Armor Panel

The portion of an armor sample that generally consists of an external carrier and its internal ballistic protective component(s) (e.g., the front and back panels).

3.4   Armor Sample

One complete armor garment comprised of a single wraparound style jacket, or a set (two) of front and back armor panels.

3.5   Backface Signature (BFS)

The depth of the depression made in the backing material, created by a nonpenetrating projectile impact, measured from the plane defined by the front edge of the backing material fixture. For armor tested on built up or curved backing material, the BFS is measured from the plane defined by the top edges of the depression or crater formed by the impact.

3.6   Backing Material

A homogenous block of nonhardening, oil base modeling clay, placed in contact with the back of the armor panel during ballistic testing.

3.7   Backing Material Fixture

A box fixture containing the backing material, typically comprised of a rigid frame constructed of wood or metal with a removable wooden back. The wooden back is not used during Ballistic Limit testing.

3.8   Baseline Ballistic Limit

The experimentally derived, statistically calculated impact velocity at which a projectile is expected to completely penetrate an armor component (sample, panel or ballistic panel) 50 % of the time (V_{50}). This velocity is also the velocity at which a projectile is expected to be stopped by the armor 50 % of the time (V_{50}).

3.9   Ballistic Panel

The protective component of an armor sample or panel, primarily consisting of ballistic resistant materials, usually enclosed in a nonremovable cover. The ballistic panel is normally retained within the armor sample or panel by a separate fabric carrier, and may be removable from the carrier.

3.10   Certification of Compliance

Manufacturer's affidavit (certification) that a production unit of body armor meets (complies with) all of the requirements of this standard (sec. 4.0) for the labeled protection classification (sec. 2.0).

3.11   Compliance

NIJ approval, after successful ballistic performance testing to this standard, of a body armor model submitted to the NIJ Compliance Testing Program (CTP).

3.12   Compliance Test Group

A group of armor samples, either six, four, or nine complete garments, submitted to the NIJ CTP for testing according to this standard (sec. 4.7).

3.13   Deformation

The maximum momentary displacement of the rear surface of an armor panel, caused by a fair hit that does not penetrate the armor, when the armor is in initial contact with the backing material.

3.14   Fair Hit

A bullet that impacts the armor sample or panel at an angle of incidence no greater than $\pm 5^\circ$ from the intended angle of incidence, no closer to the edge of the ballistic panel than 76 mm (3.0 in) and no closer to a prior hit than 51 mm (2.0 in), at an impact velocity within ± 9.1 m/s (30 ft/s) of the required reference test velocity.

A bullet that impacts the armor sample or panel at an angle of incidence no greater than $\pm 5^\circ$ from the intended angle of incidence, no closer to the edge of the ballistic panel than 76 mm (3.0 in) and no closer to a prior hit than 51 mm (2.0 in), at an impact velocity <u>less than</u> 7.6 m/s (30 ft/s) <u>below</u> the required reference test velocity <u>which produces</u> a penetration or an excessive backface signature.

A bullet that impacts the armor sample or panel at an angle of incidence no greater than $\pm 5^\circ$ from the intended angle of incidence, no closer to the edge of the ballistic panel than 76 mm (3.0 in) and no closer to a prior hit than 51 mm (2.0 in), at an impact velocity <u>more than</u> 7.6 m/s (30 ft/s) <u>above</u> the required reference test velocity <u>which does not produce</u> a penetration or an excessive backface signature.

3.15   Full Metal Jacketed Bullet (FMJ)

A bullet consisting of a lead core completely covered, except for the base, with copper alloy (approximately 90 % copper and 10 % zinc). "Total Metal Jacket (TMJ)," "Totally Enclosed Metal Case (TEMC)," and other commercial terminology for bullets with electro deposited copper and copper alloy coatings have been tested and are considered comparable to Full Metal Jacketed (FMJ) bullets for this standard.

3.16   Insert

A removable or nonremovable unit of ballistic material which can be part of either the armor or ballistic panel, which is utilized to enhance the ballistic performance of an armor in a specific area (also known as "trauma packs" or "trauma plates").

3.17 Jacketed Hollow Point Bullet (JHP)

A bullet consisting of a lead core which has a hollow cavity or hole located in the nose of the bullet and is completely covered except for the hollow point with a copper alloy (approximately 90 % copper and 10 % zinc) jacket.

3.18 Jacketed Soft Point Bullet (JSP)

A lead bullet, also known as a Semi Jacketed Soft Point (SJSP), completely covered, except for the point, with copper alloy (approximately 90 % copper and 10 % zinc) jacket.

3.19 Lead Bullet

A bullet made entirely of lead, which may be alloyed with hardening agents.

3.20 Minimum Velocity

The designated NIJ Standard–0101.04 reference impact velocity (sec.5.4, table 1) less 9.1 m/s (30 ft/s).

3.21 Model

A manufacturer's designation (name, number, or other description) that serves to uniquely identify a specific configuration of body armor based upon the details of the ballistic panel construction (i.e., the number of layers of one or more types of ballistic resistant material assembled in a specific manner or the manner in which the armor is held in place upon the torso).

NIJ verifies the ballistic resistance of a **model** based on ballistic testing of **model** samples in accordance with this standard. As an example, differences in stitching (e.g., box stitch versus quilt stitch) would make the ballistic panels different **models.** If a **model** of armor fails compliance testing, the manufacturer may never resubmit any armor under that model designation.

3.22 Obliquity

The same determination of striking condition as "angle of incidence" (sec. 3.1).

3.23 Penetration

Complete Penetration (CP): The complete perforation of an armor sample or panel by a test bullet or by a fragment of the bullet or armor sample itself, as evidenced by the presence of that bullet or fragment (armor or bullet) in the backing material, or by a hole which passes through the armor and/or backing material.

Partial Penetration (PP): Any impact that is not a complete penetration is considered a partial penetration.

3.24   Reference Bullet Velocity

The designated impact velocity of NIJ Standard–0101.04 test threat ammunition (sec. 5.4, table 1), obtained using specified ANSI/SAAMI unvented velocity test barrels.

3.25   Retest

The NIJ CTP procedure for resolving ballistic performance issues with NIJ Standard–0101.04 compliant body armor models (sec. 5.22).

3.26   Round Nose Bullet (RN)

A bullet with a blunt or rounded nose. A bullet with a generally blunt or rounded nose or tip, which possesses a small flat surface at the tip of the bullet shall also be considered a round nose bullet for this standard.

3.27   Semi Jacketed Hollow Point Bullet (SJHP)

A bullet consisting of a lead core with a copper alloy (approximately 90 % copper and 10 % zinc) jacket covering the base and bore riding surface (major diameter), which leaves some portion of the lead core exposed, thus forming a lead nose or tip, which has a hollow cavity or hole located in the nose or tip of the bullet.

3.28   Semi Jacketed Soft Point Bullet (SJSP)

A bullet, also known as a Jacketed Soft Point (JSP), consisting of a lead core with a copper alloy (approximately 90 % copper and 10 % zinc) jacket covering the base and bore riding surface (major diameter), which leaves some portion of the lead core exposed, thus forming a lead nose or tip.

3.29   Strike Face

The surface of an armor sample or panel, designated by the manufacturer, as the surface that should face the incoming ballistic threat.

3.30   Wear Face

The surface of an armor sample or panel, designated by the manufacturer, as the surface that should be worn against the body.

3.31   Yaw

The angular deviation of the longitudinal axis of the projectile from its line of flight, measured as close to the target as practical.

4. REQUIREMENTS

4.1 Acceptance Criteria

An armor model satisfies the requirements of this standard if all six armor samples (sec. 4.7) meet workmanship (sec. 4.3) and labeling (sec. 4.5) requirements and, when tested in accordance with section 5.0, each component part of the armor sample (front, back, side, groin and coccyx) meets the penetration and backface signature requirements of sections 4.6, 5.4, and table 1.

Each submitted armor sample will also be tested to determine a baseline Ballistic Limit velocity (sec. 5.17), to be used for any future NIJ retest examination of that armor model (sec. 5.22).

4.2 Test Sequence

Tests shall be conducted in the order presented in section 5.0 of this standard. The Compliance Test Report (CTR), found in appendix A, shall be used to record and document the results of the tests.

4.3 Workmanship

Each armor sample shall be free from wrinkles, blisters, cracks or fabric tears, crazing, chipped or sharp corners and edges, or other evidence of inferior workmanship. Additionally, all samples shall be identical in appearance, size, and manner of construction.

4.4 Traceability

Manufacturers will submit along with their samples, or have on file with NIJ's CTP Office, documentation of the method(s) they use to assure configuration control, uniformity of production methods, and materials traceability.

4.5 Labeling

Each set or sample of ballistic resistant armor shall be durably and clearly marked (labeled), in a readable type and font size, in accordance with the requirements set forth below.

4.5.1 Ballistic Panels

Every ballistic panel shall have a label. The label shall be permanently attached to either exterior surface of the panel. The label shall contain the following information, written in the English language (fig. 2.):

(a) Name, logo or other identification of the manufacturer.
(b) The rated level of protection, according to section 2.0 of this standard, and referenced to this edition of the standard (i.e., Type II in accordance with NIJ Standard–0101.04).
(c) Size (if custom fitted, provision for the name of the individual for whom it is made).
(d) Lot number.

(e) Date of manufacture.

(f) Date of issue line (to be filled in by user).

(g) A model designation that uniquely identifies the panel for purchasing purposes (panels designed to fit the male and female torsos shall have separate model designations).

(h) Strike face or wear face - the surface of the garment that is to face the threat or to be worn next to the body must be identified.

(i) Serial number.

(j) Care instructions for the ballistic material in accordance with 16 CFR 423 (Part 423, Care Labeling of Textile Wearing Apparel and Certain Piece Goods, as amended effective January 2, 1984; Federal Trade Commission Regulation Rule).

(k) For Type I through Type IIIA armor, a warning in type at least <u>twice</u> the size of the rest of the type on the label, exclusive of the information required in "a" above, stating that the armor is not intended to protect the wearer from rifle fire and, if applicable, that the armor is not intended to protect the wearer from sharp edged or pointed instruments. (Note: printing color changes are acceptable but cannot be substituted for the type size requirement herein).

(l) For armor that has been successfully tested for compliance to this standard through NIJ's voluntary CTP at an NIJ-approved testing facility, the following statement shall be included on the label: *"The Manufacturer certifies that this model of armor has been tested through NLECTC and has been found to comply with Type (insert appropriate type designation) Performance for NIJ Standard–0101.04."*

(m) **THE COMPLIANCE STATEMENT ABOVE SHALL NOT APPEAR ON ARMOR THAT HAS FAILED NIJ COMPLIANCE TESTING, OR ON ARMOR THAT HAS NOT BEEN TESTED FOR COMPLIANCE AS SPECIFIED BY THIS STANDARD. ONCE AUTHORIZED TO PLACE THIS STATEMENT ON A MODEL OF ARMOR, THE MANUFACTURER SHALL NOT ALTER OR MODIFY THIS STATEMENT IN ANY WAY.**

MANUFACTURER'S NAME

MANUFACTURER'S ADDRESS

(Logo may be used)

PERSONAL BODY ARMOR

SIZE: _____   MODEL: _____
DATE OF MFG: _____   SERIAL NO.: _____
DATE OF ISSUE: _____   LOT NO.: _____

The Manufacturer certifies that this model of armor has been tested through NLECTC and has been found to comply with Type II Performance in accordance with NIJ Standard—0101.04.

WARNING!

This Garment is Rated ONLY for the Ballistic Threat Level Stated Above. It is NOT Intended to Protect Against Rifle Fire, or Sharp Edged or Pointed Instruments.

THIS SIDE TO BE WORN AWAY FROM BODY

Care Instructions for Ballistic Panel: *(Sample Instructions Shown)*
1) Do Not Wash or Dry Clean
2) Wipe With a Damp Cloth

Figure 2. Sample ballistic panel label

4.5.2 Armor Carriers with Nonremovable Ballistic Panels

Armor with ballistic panels that are nonremovable shall, in addition to the label required for the ballistic panel, have a label on the carrier (fig.3) that is in conformance with the requirements for the ballistic panels (sec. 4.5.1) unless the armor is so constructed that the ballistic panel label is not covered by the carrier.

4.5.3 Armor Carriers with Removable Ballistic Panels

Armor carriers with removable ballistic panels shall have label(s) on either exterior surface of the carrier. If the carrier is one piece (i.e., all parts are sewn together into one garment) one label in conformance with the requirements of this section is sufficient. If the front and back of the carrier are separable, the front and back parts shall each be labeled. The label shall contain the following information (fig. 3):

(a) Name, logo or other identification of the manufacturer.
(b) A statement telling the user to look at the ballistic panels to determine the level of ballistic protection.

10

(c) Size (if custom fitted, provision for the name of the individual for whom it is made to be filled in by user).

(d) Date of issue line (to be filled in by user).

(e) A model designation that uniquely identifies the garment for purchasing purposes (armor designed to fit the male and female torso shall have separate model designations).

(f) For armors where the carrier extends beyond the ballistic panel more than 40 mm (1.5 in), the edge of the panel shall be clearly identified on the carrier by a label stating: "NO BALLISTIC PROTECTION BEYOND THIS POINT" (fig.4), and a stitch line through both sides of the carrier at this location to keep the ballistic panel from shifting within the carrier.

(g) Care instructions for the armor carrier in accordance with 16 CFR 423.

MANUFACTURERS NAME
MANUFACTURER'S ADDRESS
(Logo may be used)

PERSONAL BODY ARMOR

NAME: _____

SIZE: _____   **MODEL:** _____

DATE OF MFG: _____   **SERIAL NO.:** _____

DATE OF ISSUE: _____   **LOT NO.:** _____

This carrier offers no ballistic protection without ballistic panels being inserted.
See ballistic panel labels for protection level provided in accordance with
NIJ Standard–0101.04.

CARE INSTRUCTIONS FOR CARRIER:
(sample instructions shown – to be provided by Manufacturer)

1)   Remove Ballistic Panels from Front and Back of Outer Shell Vest (Carrier).
2)   Ensure Hook and Pile Fasteners are in Closed Position during Washing Cycle.
3)   Automatic Machine Wash the Outer Shell Vest (Carrier) Only, Using the Permanent Press Cycle and Warm Water Settings (Approximately 120 °F).
4)   Use Low Sudsing Detergent According to Detergent Manufacturer's Directions.
5)   DO NOT USE BLEACH.
6)   Carrier Only may be Tumble Dried at Medium Temperature Setting or may be Line Dried.
7)   Carrier Only may be Dry Cleaned.
8)   Carrier Must be Completely Dry Before Inserting Ballistic Panels.

Figure 3. Sample carrier label

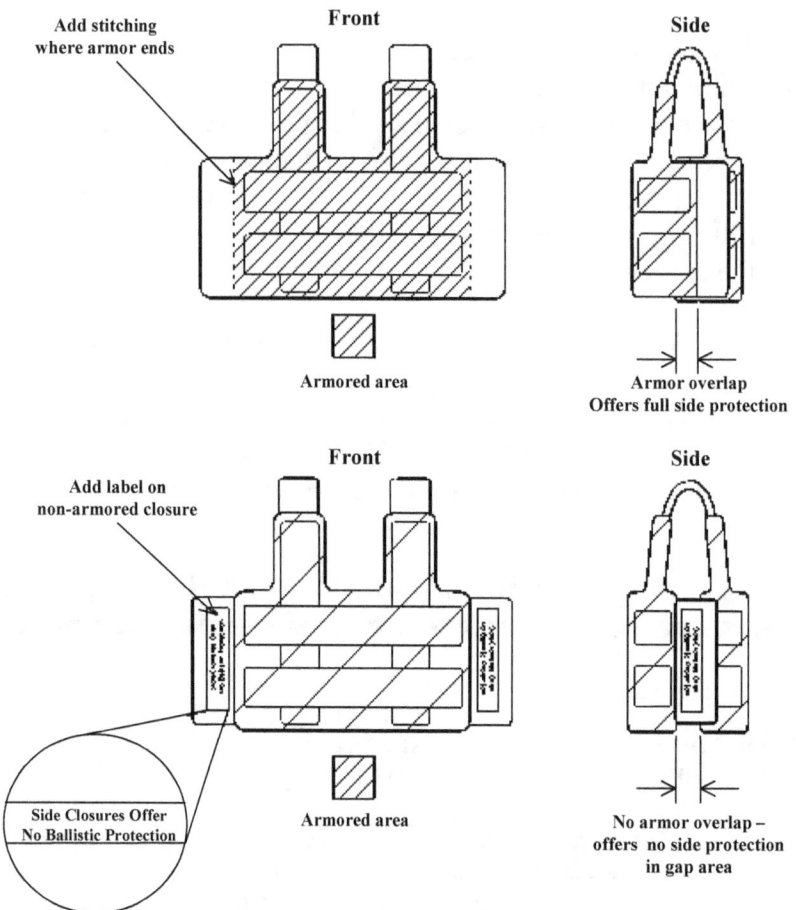

Figure 4. Sample label locations

4.5.4 Armors with Built In Trauma Packs

For armor models that contain built in inserts or trauma packs, manufacturers must submit a detailed diagram of the location of each trauma pack. If a manufacturer fails to notify the NIJ CTP Office of the existence of a built in insert or trauma pack and it is discovered during testing, the test results for that model will be invalidated. The manufacturer may resubmit the model for testing under the same model designation after resolving the lack of documentation concerning the location of the insert or trauma pack.

4.6 Ballistic Penetration and Backface Signature Criteria

Each part of one complete body armor sample shall be tested for resistance to ballistic penetration and backface signature (depth of depression in backing material) after wet conditioning in accordance with the procedures in section 5.0. Complete penetration or any designated depth measurement of BFS in the backing material greater than 44 mm (1.73 in) by any fair hit (as defined in sec. 3.14) shall constitute a failure.

12

If any armor sample part fails at any time during compliance testing, data for that shot shall be recorded and the testing continued until all required testing is completed. The detailed test requirements are summarized in section 5.4, table 1. Type I, IIA, II, or IIIA armor designed to include a removable insert for additional penetration or BFS protection over a localized area of the armor sample or panel shall be tested without the insert.

4.7   Sampling

4.7.1   Types I, IIA, II, and IIIA

Six complete armors, sized to fit a 117 cm (46 in) to 122 cm (48 in) chest circumference for males and a 107 cm (42 in) to 112 cm (44 in) chest circumference for females, shall constitute the compliance test group. Five of these armor samples shall be selected at random from the group and used for ballistic testing. Four armor samples will be used for Penetration and Backface Signature testing (sec. 5.4), and one armor sample will be used for baseline Ballistic Limit determination (sec. 5.17). The remaining armor sample will be returned to the manufacturer if not used in the ballistic testing.

4.7.2   Type III

Four complete armor samples, or panels, no smaller than 254 mm x 305 mm (10.0 in x 12.0 in) shall constitute a compliance test group. Two of these armor samples shall be selected at random from the group and used for the testing. Two armors will be used for Penetration and Backface Signature testing, and at least one armor sample will be used for baseline Ballistic Limit determination (sec. 5.17). Any remaining armor samples will be returned to the manufacturer if not used in the ballistic testing.

4.7.3   Type IV

Nine complete armor samples/panels/inserts, no smaller than 203 mm x 254 mm (8.0 in x 10.0 in) shall constitute a compliance test group. Eight of these armor samples shall be selected at random and used for the testing. Two armor samples will be used for Penetration and Backface Signature testing, and at least six complete armor samples will be used for baseline Ballistic Limit determination (sec. 5.17). Any remaining armor samples will be returned to the manufacturer if not used in the testing.

4.8   Armor Backing Material

4.8.1   Backing Material Fixture (BMF)

A minimum of three Backing Material Fixtures filled with appropriate backing material are required. The inside dimensions of the BMF shall be 610 mm x 610 mm x 140 mm ± 2 mm (24.0 in x 24.0 in x 5.5 in ± 0.06 in) deep. The tolerance on all dimensions will be ± 2 mm (0.06 in).

The back of the fixture shall be removable and constructed of 19.1 mm (0.75 in) thick wood or plywood.

4.8.2   Fixture Construction

The sides of the box fixture shall be constructed of rigid wood or metal, preferably with a metal front edge to reliably guide the preparation of the flat front surface of the backing material. The backing material shall be worked into the fixture (box) with as few voids as possible. The backing material surface shall be cut, "struck," or otherwise manipulated to result in a smooth, flat front surface even with the front edges of the box fixture.

4.8.3   Backing Material

It has been determined that Roma Plastilina No.1[1] oil-based modeling clay is acceptable for the backing material application. In the interest of conformity only, it is being specified as the designated backing material for all NIJ Standard–0101.04 Body Armor Compliance Testing. This material is available from art supply stores.

4.8.4   Backing Material Replacement and Identification

Clay used as backing material in NIJ Compliance Testing shall be replaced on an annual basis as a minimum, and the replacement date shall be recorded on the backing material fixture.

4.9   Test Surveillance

NIJ representatives may witness compliance testing at any time. NIJ or its designated representatives shall be afforded the opportunity to examine the range and test setup before beginning any new series of compliance testing. The manufacturer shall inform NIJ CTP personnel of the intent to test at least two weeks before the start of testing.

---

[1]The use of brand names in this standard does not constitute endorsement by the U.S. Department of Justice; National Institute of Justice; U.S. Department of Commerce; National Institute of Standards and Technology; Office of Law Enforcement Standards; or any other agency of the United States Federal Government, nor does it imply that the product is best suited for its intended applications.

4.10   Compliance Test Documentation

All NIJ compliance testing will be formally documented using the CTR found in appendix A. Submission of this form will be made to the NIJ CTP Office within 10 working days following the completion of testing.

5. TEST METHODS

5.1   Purpose

This section constitutes the formal test procedure for Penetration and Backface Signature (P-BFS) and baseline Ballistic Limit (BL) determination testing of personal body armor intended for use by Law Enforcement and Corrections personnel. It specifies the equipment and techniques to be used by NIJ-approved and certified testing agents to qualify voluntarily submitted body armor models for P-BFS compliance and baseline ballistic limit determination.

To achieve NIJ compliance to this standard, each submitted armor model must successfully complete a two-part performance test series. The first test series, P-BFS, is designed to measure the overall ballistic performance of the armor according to pass/fail criteria (sec. 4.6). The second test series, baseline BL determination, is a test to penetration failure and is designed to statistically measure penetration performance (sec. 5.17). No pass/fail criteria are attached to the BL portion of the testing.

5.2   Sampling

Five armor samples will be selected at random from the compliance test group for ballistic testing.

5.3   References

The following references form a basis for and support the procedures described in this section:

[1] National Institute of Justice. NIJ Standard–0101.03, *Ballistic Resistance of Police Body Armor* (1987).

[2] American National Standards Institute. SAAMI Z299.1–1992, *Voluntary Industry Standards for Pressure and Velocity of Centerfire Rifle Sporting Ammunition for the Use of Commercial Manufacturers.*

[3] American National Standards Institute. SAAMI Z299.3–1993, *Voluntary Industry Standards for Pressure and Velocity of Centerfire Pistol and Revolver Ammunition for the Use of Commercial Manufacturers.*

[4] American National Standards Institute. SAAMI Z299.4–1992, *Voluntary Industry Standards for Pressure and Velocity of Rimfire Sporting Ammunition for the Use of Commercial Manufacturers.*

[5] Department of Defense. MIL–STD–662F, *DoD Test Method Standard, V50 Ballistic Test for Armor.* (1997).

[6] U.S. Army Test and Evaluation Command. TOP 2–2–710, *Test Operations Procedure, Ballistic Tests of Armor Materials.* (1984), or latest version.

5.4 Ballistic Penetration and Backface Signature Test (P-BFS)

All armor models submitted to NIJ for compliance testing will undergo a series of ballistic impact tests using the ammunition (threat rounds) specified in section 5.4, table 1. These impact tests measure two Backface Signatures (BFS) and demonstrate the armor's pass/fail penetration capability. This test series requires the use of a plastically deforming witness media (clay backing material) held in direct contact with the back surface of the armor panel. This configuration is used to capture and measure the BFS depression produced in the backing material during nonperforating threat round impacts.

The use of clay backing material and the subsequent BFS depth measurement does not reflect, represent, replicate, or duplicate the physical characteristics of the human torso or its physical response to this type of stimulus.

5.4.1 Handloads

With the exception of the .22 caliber Long Rifle threat round, handloads may be used in P-BFS tests. The bullets shall be as specified in appendix D. Verification of the handload velocity for each threat round will require firing at least 10 shots per threat caliber prior to each compliance test series. The arithmetic mean of the 10 shot handload series shall be within ± 3 m/s (10 ft/s) of the reference velocities specified in section 5.4, table 1. Individual shots within the 10 shot group may vary up to ± 9 m/s (30 ft/s) from the reference velocity. The results of the handload velocity tests shall be recorded where indicated in the CTR.

5.4.2 Test Weapons

The test weapons shall be ANSI/SAAMI unvented velocity test barrels. No firearms will be used (with the possible exception of Type Special).

5.4.3 Test Weapon Fixtures

The ANSI/SAAMI test barrels will be mounted in an ANSI/SAAMI Universal Receiver (sec. 5.3, Ref. [2]) or in an alternative NIJ-approved substitute mounting fixture. The receiver/mount will be attached to a table or other fixture having sufficient mass and restraint to ensure accurate targeting of repetitively fired rounds. Test barrels may be fabricated without the Universal Receiver collar to permit use of alternative mounting devices.

Table 1. NIJ Standard–0101.04 P-BFS performance test summary

Armor Type	Test Round	Test Bullet	Bullet Weight	Reference Velocity (± 30 ft/s)	Hits Per Armor Part at 0° Angle of Incidence	BFS Depth Maximum	Hits Per Armor Part at 30° Angle of Incidence	Shots Per Panel	Shots Per Sample	Shots Per Threat	Total Shots Req'd
I	1	.22 caliber LR LRN	2.6 g 40 gr.	329 m/s (1080 ft/s)	4	44 mm (1.73 in)	2	6	12	24	48
	2	.380 ACP FMJ RN	6.2 g 95 gr.	322 m/s (1055 ft/s)	4	44mm (1.73 in)	2	6	12	24	
IIA	1	9 mm FMJ RN	8.0 g 124 gr.	341 m/s (1120 ft/s)	4	44 mm (1.73 in)	2	6	12	24	48
	2	40 S&W FMJ	11.7 g 180 gr.	322 m/s (1055 ft/s)	4	44 mm (1.73 in)	2	6	12	24	
II	1	9 mm FMJ RN	8.0 g 124 gr.	367 m/s (1205 ft/s)	4	44 mm (1.73 in)	2	6	12	24	48
	2	357 Mag JSP	10.2 g 158 gr.	436 m/s (1430 ft/s)	4	44 mm (1.73 in)	2	6	12	24	
IIIA	1	9 mm FMJ RN	8.2 g 124 gr.	436 m/s (1430 ft/s)	4	44 mm (1.73 in)	2	6	12	24	48
	2	44 Mag JHP	15.6 g 240 gr.	436 m/s (1430 ft/s)	4	44 mm (1.73 in)	2	6	12	24	
III	1	7.62 mm NATO FMJ	9.6 g 148 gr.	838 m/s (2780 ft/s)	6	44 mm (1.73 in)	0	6	12	12	12
IV	1	.30 caliber M2 AP	10.8 g 166 gr.	869 m/s (2880 ft/s)	1	44 mm (1.73 in)	0	1	2	2	2
Special	*	*	*	*	*	44 mm (1.73 in)	*	*	*	*	*

Panel = Front or back component of typical armor sample.

Sample = Full armor garment, including all component panels (F & B).

Threat = Test ammunition round by caliber.

5.5 Velocity Measurement Equipment

5.5.1 Requirements

Test round velocities will be determined using two independent sets of instrumentation. Velocities from each set of instrumentation will be recorded, and the arithmetic mean of the two velocities will be calculated and recorded. The measured individual test velocities recorded from each set shall be within 3 m/s (10 ft/s) of each other to be considered a fair velocity. If the specified correlation is not achieved, the test velocity shall be that obtained from the widest instrument spacing (as applicable).

5.5.2 Equipment

Recommended types of equipment for velocity measurement are:

(a) Photo electric light screens.
(b) Printed make circuit screens.
(c) Printed break circuit screens.
(d) Ballistic radar.

Independent sets of velocity measurement may be obtained using two pairs of photo electric light screens, two sets of make screens, two sets of break screens, or any paired set combination. Chronographs, A→B counters, storage scopes, or other digital instruments used to record the measurement equipment's signals will, as a minimum, be capable of recording to 0.3 m/s (1.0 ft/s), or one tenth (0.1) of one μs (10^{-6} s).

5.5.3 Configuration

The first chronograph start trigger screen will be placed a minimum of 2 m $\pm$ 3 mm (78.7 in $\pm$ 0.12 in) from the muzzle of the test barrel (sec. 5.10.2, fig. 6). The screens will be arranged so that they define vertical planes perpendicular to the line of flight of the bullet. The screens will be securely mounted to maintain their required position and spacing (measurement accuracy of $\pm$ 1 mm ($\pm$ 0.04 in).

5.5.4 Calibration

Velocity measuring instrumentation will be calibrated according to the manufacturer's instructions. Calibration shall be accomplished at the following intervals:

(a) Prior to any NIJ laboratory certification for compliance testing.
(b) Prior to any NIJ recertification of the testing laboratory.
(c) As recommended by the equipment manufacturer.
(d) Annually.

5.5.5 Calibration Records

Test instrumentation calibration records will be maintained and made available to the NIJ CTP upon request. All calibration procedures and values will be traceable to NIST requirements.

5.6 Wet Conditioning

5.6.1 Environmental Condition

Body armor undergoing P-BFS performance testing will be tested in a wet condition. This condition will be produced by exposing the armor panel under test to a specified flow and distribution of water prior to beginning the ballistic testing (sec. 5.6.2).

5.6.2 Spray Conditioning Equipment

The minimum conditioning surface area of the spray enclosure will be 762 mm x 762 mm (30.0 in x 30.0 in). This surface should be constructed of a material that will permit the unobstructed flow of water through it, without allowing build-up on the spray facing surface. The enclosure will be constructed in such a manner that the flow of water cannot accumulate, to prevent complete immersion of the armor panel. A single spray nozzle will be mounted in the top of the enclosure.

5.6.3 Conditioning Requirements

The average flow rate from the spray nozzle shall be 100 mm/h ± 20 mm/h (4.0 in/h ± 0.8 in/h), determined by calculating the arithmetic mean of five rain gauges symmetrically arranged within the prescribed conditioning surface area (sec. 5.6.4, b). The source water temperature will be 10 $^\circ$C to 21 $^\circ$C (50 $^\circ$F to 70 $^\circ$F).

5.6.4 Spray Conditioning Calibration

The spray conditioning system will be calibrated once daily during all compliance test series. Calibration will be completed prior to beginning any armor sample conditioning, using the methodology and equipment described below. Spray calibration results will be recorded in the CTR (app. A).

(a) Divide the conditioning surface area (sec. 5.6.2) into four equal quadrants, permanently marking the center of each quadrant, and the center of all four quadrants.
(b) In the center of each quadrant, and at the center of the four quadrants, place a rain gauge capable of measuring increments of 2.5 mm (0.1 in) or better (five gauges total). A one piece design consisting of five gauges attached to a metal cross frame has been shown to work well.
(c) Time the conditioning event using a stopwatch capable of 1 s measurement intervals. A minimum duration of 15 min will be used to establish the flow rate, measured using the five rain gauges.
(d) Inspect the gauges and record the level of water at each location. Calculate the arithmetic mean of the five water levels. The calibration results will be recorded on the CTR.

(e) If the calculated arithmetic mean flow rate, measured in each quadrant and at the center of the quadrants, is not within specified tolerances, the calibration process must be repeated until the specifications are met.

5.7   Backing Material Fixture Preparation

5.7.1   Backing Material Fixtures (BMF)

The fixtures will conform to the requirements in section 4.8.

5.7.2   Surface Preparation

The clay in each BMF will be manipulated to produce a block free of voids, and with a smooth, flat front surface for the accurate and consistent measurement of depression depths. The front surface of the backing material shall be even with the surface plane defined by the fixture edges. Additional clay, conditioned along with each BMF, shall be used to fill voids and restore the front surface as needed.

5.7.3   Backing Material Conditioning

The clay backing material shall initially be conditioned in its fixture, using a heated chamber or enclosure, for at least 3 h at temperatures above 29 $^\circ$C (85 $^\circ$F). Actual conditioning temperature and recovery time between uses will be determined by drop test results (sec. 5.7.5). New backing material may require temperatures above 35 $^\circ$C (95 $^\circ$F) to consistently achieve 5.7.5 criteria. Conditioning time, temperature, and corresponding drop test performance may change as a function of backing material age and usage.

5.7.4   Conditioning Chamber

The conditioning chamber shall be constructed such that the backing material fixture(s) are positioned with adequate (152 mm (6.0 in)) spacing between them to permit even temperature soaking. The chamber shall be convective in design, with provision for continuous air circulation within the chamber during conditioning cycles.

5.7.5   Backing Material Calibration

Calibration of the Roma Plastilina #1 clay backing material will be accomplished before (pretest), and after (post test) each six shot firing sequence (sec. 5.4, table 1). Calibration will be accomplished using the equipment and techniques specified below:

(a) Drop weight: Steel Sphere.[2]
(b) Drop weight size: 63.5 mm ± 0.05 mm (2.5 in ± 0.001 in) in diameter.
(c) Drop weight mass: 1043 g ± 5 g (2.29 lb ± 0.01 lb).
(d) Drop height: 2.0 m (6.56 ft).
(e) Drop spacing: 76 mm ± 3 mm (3.0 in ± 0.125 in) from edges and 203 mm

---

[2]A sphere, reference P/N 3606, supplied by Salem Specialty Ball Co., Inc., P.O. Box 145, West Simsbury, CT 06092, has been found to be satisfactory, although any steel sphere meeting the requirements listed in this section is acceptable.

± 25 mm (8.0 in ± 1.0 in) between indent centers.

Each calibration drop will consist of a free fall of the steel sphere onto the conditioned backing material. A minimum of five drops will be completed, with the five drop arithmetic mean depth of depression to be 20 mm ± 3 mm (0.787 in ± 0.12 in). Depth of depression will be measured from the original flat surface of the prepared backing material using a depth gauge measurement tool. The general pretest drop locations will be located according to figure 5.

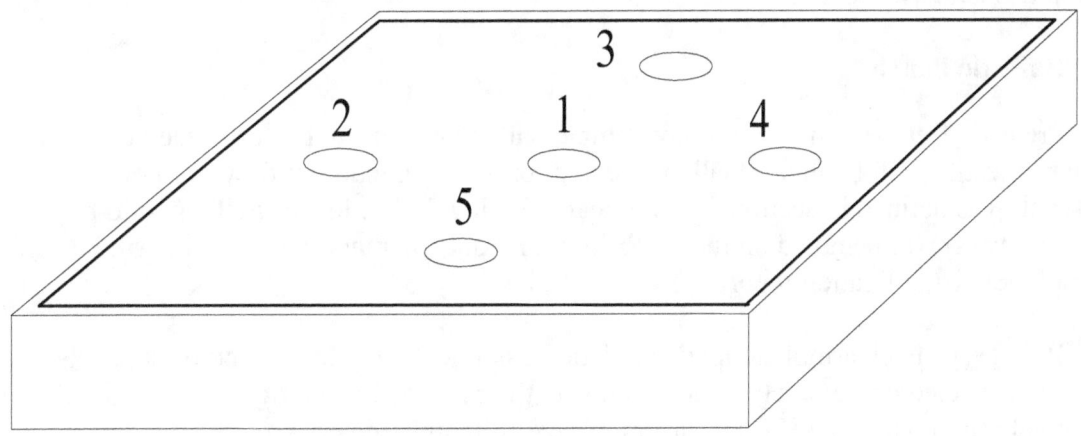

Figure 5. General pretest drop locations

5.7.6   Female Body Armor Backing Material

For body armor sized and shaped for females, the bust cups shall be built up and supported with backing material conditioned to the same temperature as the main body of the backing material and in the same manner as referenced in section 5.7; however, calibration drop testing <u>does not</u> have to be performed in the built up area.

5.7.7   Backing Material Fixture Rotation

A newly conditioned and drop test calibrated BMF will be used whenever calibration drop test results dictate. Failure to meet post test drop depth requirements (sec. 5.7.5) will result in the invalidation of the previous six shot series. All drop test calibration results will be recorded in the CTR. It is recommended that a minimum of two fixtures be rotated among the test and conditioning cycles to ensure meeting these requirements.

5.8 Workmanship Examination

5.8.1 Armor Carriers

All armor sample carriers and ballistic panel coverings received for compliance testing will be individually inspected for damage, material flaws, or poor workmanship as defined in section 4.3. All tears, fraying, holes, loose stitching, or other identified flaw(s) will be noted on the CTR form; documentary photographs will be taken for use in deficiency notification reporting (sec. 5.8.4).

5.8.2 Ballistic Panels

Pretest – Before testing, all armor sample ballistic panels and inserts received for compliance testing will be individually inspected for damage, material flaws, or poor workmanship as defined in section 4.3. All tears, fraying, holes, loose stitching, or other identified flaw(s) will be noted on the CTR form, and documentary photographs will be taken for use in deficiency notification reporting.

Post Test - Each armor sample's ballistic components (e.g., front and back panels) will be physically inspected immediately after testing and their respective configuration reported in the CTR for submission to the NIJ CTP (layers, weave, stitching, material, etc.).

5.8.3 Label Examination

The complete armor sample and each part (carrier and ballistic panels) will be examined for conformance to the labeling requirements of section 4.5. Note any deviations from requirements in the CTR.

5.8.4 Inspection Deficiency Notification

The NIJ CTP and the armor manufacturer will be notified within 24 h of discovery of any shipping damage, major product flaws, or poor quality workmanship, or label inconsistency. Notification will consist of a summary letter and documentary photographs. Such discoveries and notices will result in suspension of the compliance test until NIJ CTP resolution or approval to proceed is received by the testing laboratory.

5.9 Armor Conditioning

5.9.1 Temperature/Humidity Conditioning

All armor samples received for compliance testing shall be stored and conditioned for a minimum of 12 h at ambient range conditions (sec. 5.10.1).

5.9.2 Inserts

All armor samples will be tested in their final design and end use configuration, including all system components (e.g., carriers and straps), with the exception of removable trauma inserts/packs, which will be removed before conditioning.

5.9.3 Wet Conditioning

The complete armor panel (including removable carriers) shall be conditioned for wet armor testing by exposing it to a 6 min cycle of water spray, using the equipment and conditions specified in section 5.6. Each face of the armor panel will be laid flat upon the conditioning surface (sec. 5.6.2) and exposed to the spray for 3 min, with the strike face of the panel conditioned last. Ballistic testing shall begin immediately after the armor panel is removed from the wet conditioning chamber. If the armor is equipped with waterproof bladders or covers, they shall not be modified or altered in any way.

5.9.4 Test Duration

After wet conditioning, the duration of the six shot firing sequence for each armor panel, front or back, will be no longer than 30 min, with the first round fired within 10 min after completion of the wet conditioning cycle. If testing has not been completed in the time permitted, the test data shall be discarded and testing must begin again with a new wet conditioned armor panel. Test start and stop times will be recorded in the CTR.

5.10 Range Configuration

5.10.1 Ambient Test Conditions

Unless otherwise specified, the ambient conditions of the test range shall be:

(a) Temperature: $21\,^{\circ}C \pm 2.9\,^{\circ}C$ ($70\,^{\circ}F \pm 5\,^{\circ}F$).
(b) Relative humidity: $50\,\% \pm 20\,\%$.
(c) Range conditions will be recorded in the CTR before and after each armor sample firing sequence (12 shots).

5.10.2 Range Preparation

Set up the test equipment as shown in figure 6. Use a test barrel appropriate for the ammunition required to test the armor (sec. 5.4, table 1), mounted in an appropriate fixture with the barrel horizontal. Dimensions A and B shall be determined from the barrel muzzle. The BMF will be rigidly held by a suitable (metal) test stand, which shall permit the entire armor and backing material assembly to be shifted vertically and horizontally such that the entire assembly can be targeted by the test barrel.

5.10.3 Measurement Tolerances

Range configuration measurements A and B (fig. 6) are to be made within a tolerance of ± 25 mm (± 1.0 in).

5.10.4 Instrumentation

All electronic equipment will be turned on and allowed to warm up until stability is achieved.

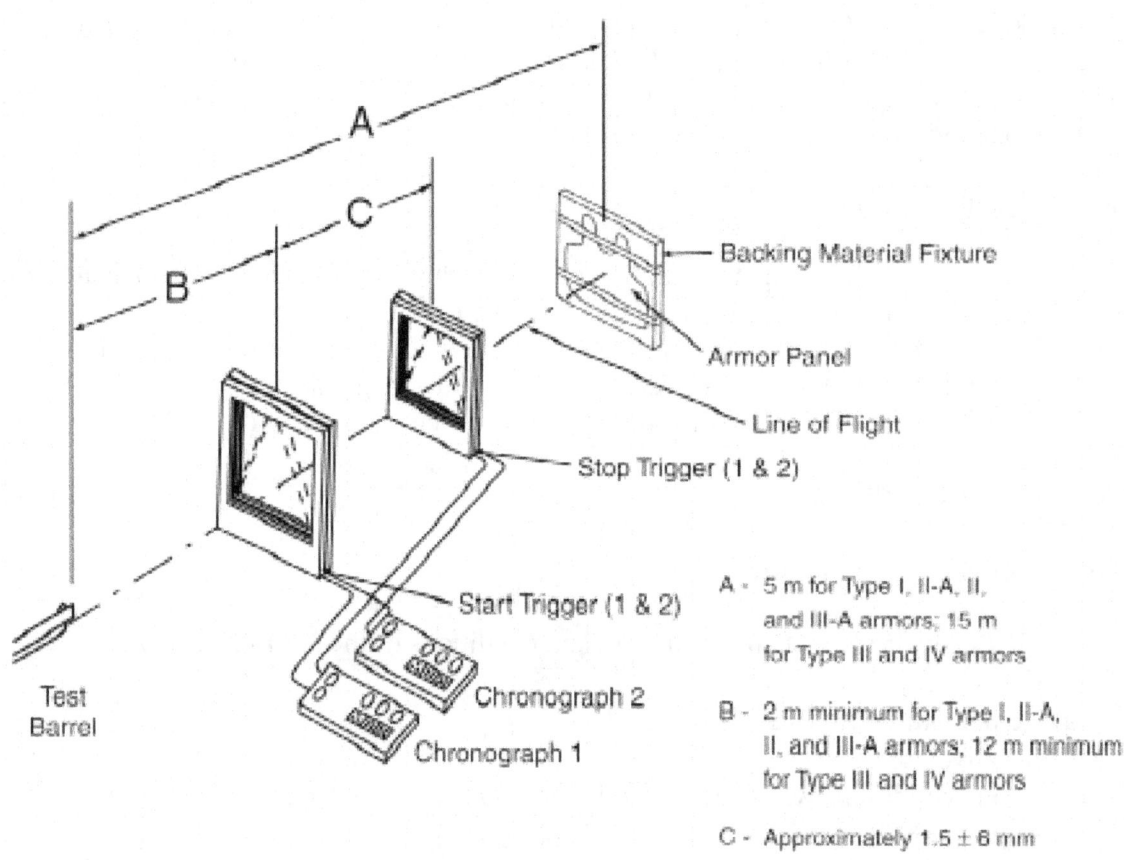

Figure 6. Test range configuration

5.11 Test Preparation

5.11.1 Test Barrel Conditioning

Select the required test bullet for the armor type as specified in section 5.4, table 1. Beginning with threat round number one, fire a minimum of three pretest rounds to ensure that the first test round fired will strike the target as aimed, using a suitable targeting device (e.g., a pointing laser). These pretest rounds will also serve to "warm" or stabilize the temperature of the barrel before further testing.

5.11.2 Handload Verification

Before the first armor panel test sequence, fire the 10 shot handload series (sec. 5.4.1) and record the result in the CTR.

5.11.3 Shot Location Marking

Clearly mark the shot locations directly on the sample (fig. 7) following the spacing criteria of section 3.14.

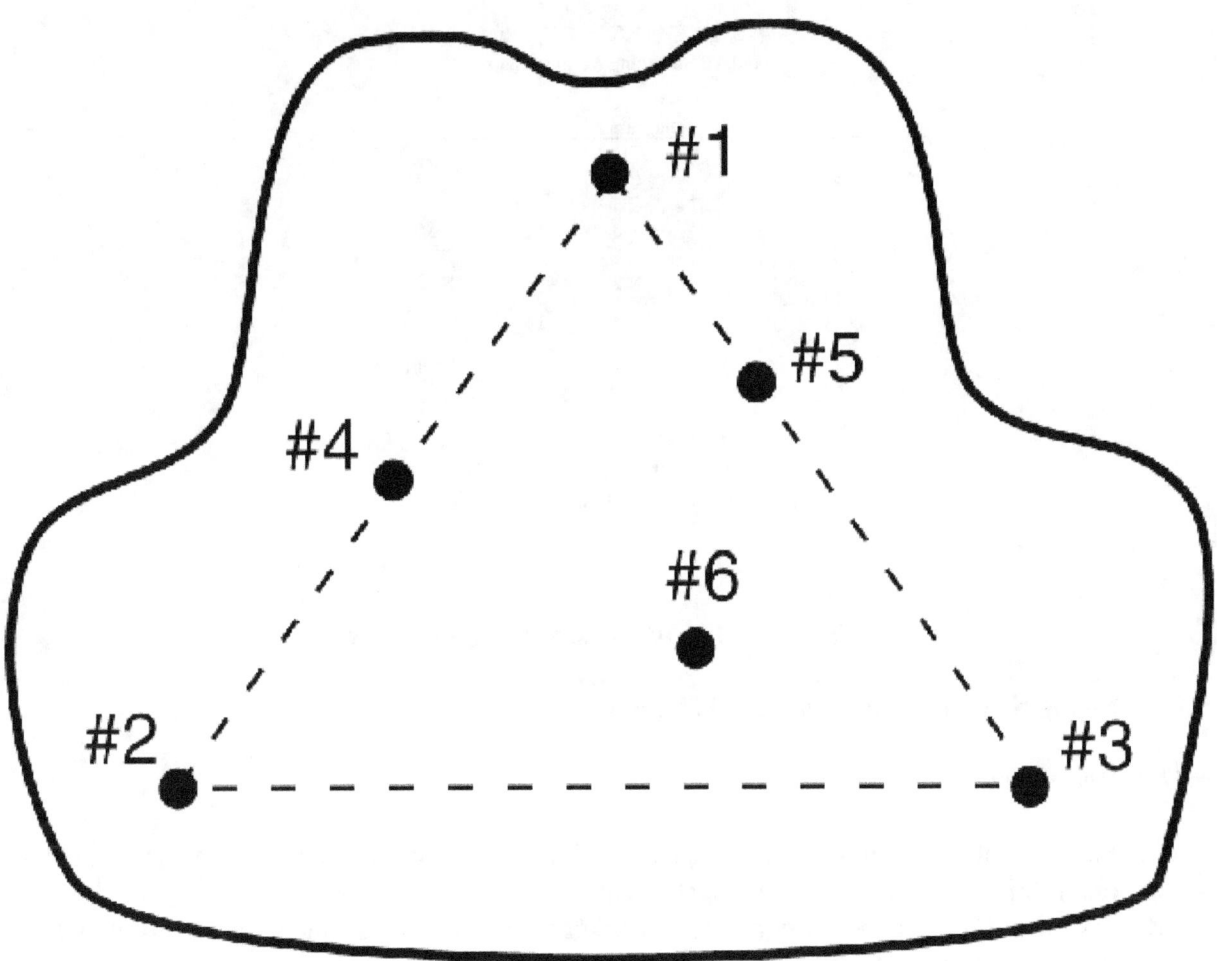

Figure 7. General armor panel impact locations (front and back)

5.11.4 Armor Strapping

Armor samples or panels will be secured to the backing material fixture using 51 mm (2.0 in) wide elastic straps, held together using Velcro® attachments. Figure 8, diagram 1 details the type and location of the strapping devices. The placement of the straps will be such that they do not interfere with the impact points on the panels.

Using a pencil or other appropriate tool, lightly trace the outline of the sample onto the backing material to document the original position of the sample.

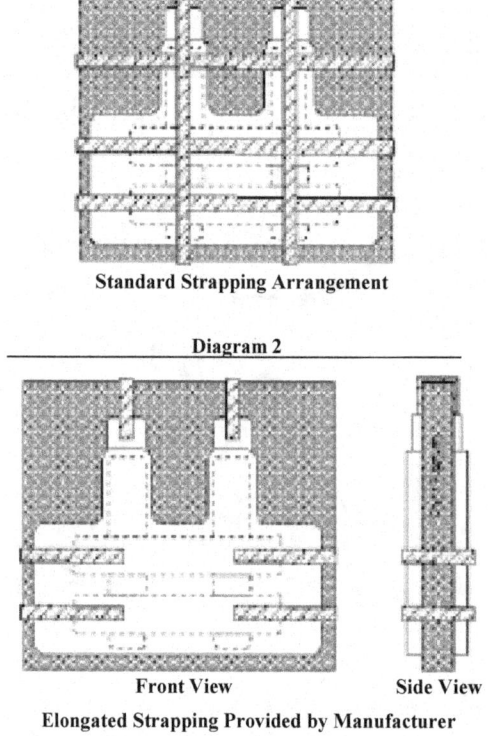

Diagram 1

Standard Strapping Arrangement

Diagram 2

Front View   Side View

Elongated Strapping Provided by Manufacturer

Figure 8. Acceptable strapping methods

5.12 Firing Sequence for Type I, IIA, II, and IIIA Armor

5.12.1 Requirements

(a) Four complete armor samples, consisting of either a front and back set of armor panels or one full jacket; two samples per test threat.

(b) Six fair hit impacts per armor panel or jacket front and back surface, four armor panels (two front and two back) or two armor jackets for each test threat, for a total of 24 impacts per test threat; and 48 total impacts per compliance test.

(c) BFS of two normal obliquity impacts in each armor panel, a total of 16 measurements per compliance test sequence. A BFS reading shall be taken at shot location No. 1 for each panel. The remaining BFS shall be taken at the shot location having the highest fair hit velocity of shot locations No. 2 and 3.

26

5.12.2 Acceptance Criteria for Penetration and BFS Compliance

(a) No perforation through the panel, either by the bullet or by any fragment of the bullet or armor.

(b) No measured BFS depression depth greater than 44 mm (1.73 in).

5.12.3 Test Range Configuration

Position the front face of the backing material 5 m ± 25 mm (16.4 ft ± 1.0 in) from the muzzle of the test barrel (fig. 6). Position the velocity measurement instrumentation according to figure 6, item B. Prepare the required test round as specified in section 5.4, table 1. Complete the handload verification requirement (sec. 5.11.2), or fire a sufficient number of pretest rounds (minimum of three) to ensure that the handloaded test round will strike the armor with a velocity within the specified velocity range. Use an appropriate aiming system to ensure proper placement of the test bullet.

5.12.4 Sample Preparation, Mounting and Firing

5.12.4.1 For armor panels sized and shaped for females, the bust cups shall be filled with backing material conditioned in the same manner as referenced in section 5.7; however, the drop test for consistency does not have to be performed in this area. Further, impact locations four or five of the shot sequence shall be such that at least one of the 30° angle of incidence shots impact on a bust cup. If the bust cup contains one or more seams, the manufacturer shall submit a detailed diagram to identify the location of each seam, and one shot shall impact a seam.

5.12.4.2 For armor employing a front opening system, shot location one shall be adjusted, if necessary, to prevent the shot from impacting a double or overlapping layer of ballistic material. Further, impact locations four and five of the shot sequence shall be adjusted such that at least one of the 30° angle of incidence shots shall impact the closure seam.

5.12.4.3 Start with the wet conditioned (sec. 5.9) front panel of armor sample 1. Place the exposed surface of the calibrated backing material in intimate contact with the backface of the armor panel under test and restrict the movement of the panel from its original position by securing it with two vertical and three horizontal elastic straps, 51 mm (2.0 in) wide with Velcro® closures, supplied by the testing laboratory (fig. 8, diagram 1). Using a pencil or other appropriate tool, lightly trace the outline of the sample onto the backing material to document the original position of the sample.

5.12.4.4 The straps shall be positioned to restrict the movement of the panel from its original position, leaving the strike face impact area(s) exposed. If the strapping is an integral part of the armor panel, the manufacturer may supply sample panels with extended strapping devices to allow the armor, as a unit, to be mounted on the backing material fixture (fig. 8, diagram 2). The laboratory shall indicate in the CTR which strapping arrangement was used.

5.12.4.5 Position the backing material fixture to assure proper impact placement and angle of incidence (0°) of the test round at location one, as shown in figure 7.

5.12.4.6 Fire Shot No. 1: Fire the first test round against the armor panel at location one (fig. 7), and record the velocity. Examine the armor panel and the backing material to determine whether the bullet made a fair hit and whether complete penetration occurred. If no complete penetration (CP) occurred and the bullet made a fair hit, measure and record the BFS depression depth after "striking" the surface of the clay to reestablish the original surface plane (if necessary to accurately measure BFS). Record the BFS on the CTR, and proceed to section 5.12.3.8.

5.12.4.7 If no complete penetration occurred and the bullet made an unfair hit, a second attempt will be made to attain a fair hit. This second attempt will be made to impact the same general area of the armor as the first shot but more than 51 mm (2.0 in) from the previous shot and more than 76 mm (3.0 in) from any edge of the panel. If a fair hit is still not attained, the firing sequence will be terminated and a new armor panel prepared in accordance with section 5.9. The firing sequence will then be repeated using the newly conditioned panel of armor. No more than a total of eight impacts is permitted on any armor panel.

5.12.4.8 Remount Armor Sample: Adjust the armor panel back to its original condition (i.e., smooth and manipulate the ballistic material to return it to its original configuration) and replace it on the backing material in its original position using the traced outline in the backing material as a guide. Do not recondition the backing material; do not repair the BFS depression in the backing material; do not remove the test bullet if it is trapped in the panel. When conducting the remaining firing sequence, inspect the armor panel following each impact to verify that the impact was a fair hit with no complete penetration, and smooth out the panel in preparation for the next shot.

5.12.4.9 Fire Shot No. 2: Reposition the backing material fixture with the armor panel in position so that the shot will impact the panel at location two (fig. 7). Fire the test round. Do not change the position of the armor panel on the backing material, but adjust the panel and mounting straps as necessary to restore its original condition. Do not remove any trapped bullets from the panel and do not disturb the BFS depressions in the backing material.

5.12.4.10 Fire Shot No. 3: Reposition the backing material fixture with the armor panel in position so that the shot will impact the panel at location three (fig. 7). Fire the test round. Do not change the position of the armor panel on the backing material, but adjust the panel and mounting straps as necessary to restore its original condition. Do not remove any trapped bullets from the panel and do not disturb the BFS depressions in the backing material.

5.12.4.11 Fire Shot No. 4: Reposition the backing material fixture so that the defined angle of incidence between the perpendicular to the armor panel and the line of flight of the test round is $30°$ (fig. 1), ensuring the bullet will be directed toward the center of the armor panel, such that the bullet will impact the armor at location four (fig. 7). Fire the test round. Do not change the position of the armor panel on the backing material, but adjust the panel and mounting straps as necessary to restore its original condition. Do not remove any trapped bullets from the panel and do not disturb the BFS depressions in the backing material.

5.12.4.12   Fire Shot No. 5: Reposition the backing material fixture so that the defined angle of incidence between the perpendicular to the armor panel and the line of flight of the test round is 30° (fig. 1), ensuring the bullet will be directed toward the center of the armor panel, such that the bullet will impact the armor at location five (fig. 7). Fire the test round. Do not change the position of the armor panel on the backing material, but adjust the panel and mounting straps as necessary to restore its original condition. Do not remove any trapped bullets from the panel and do not disturb the BFS depressions in the backing material.

5.12.4.13   Fire Shot No. 6: Reposition the backing material fixture with the armor panel in position so that the defined angle of incidence between the perpendicular to the armor and the line of flight of the test round is 0° (fig. 1) and the bullet will impact the armor at location six (fig. 7). Fire the test round. Remove and thoroughly examine the armor panel and backing material for complete penetrations by bullets or fragments.

5.12.4.14   Measure Second BFS: Identify the highest velocity fair hit impact of shots two and three. Strike the backing material surface to reestablish the original surface plane (as necessary) and measure the BFS depth of the selected highest velocity fair hit impact using a depth measuring tool (sec. 5.12.3.6). Record this BFS on the CTR.

5.12.4.15   Post Test Drop Calibration: Without repairing the BFS depressions from the firing sequence, perform five drop tests on the backing material in the general areas of figure 5. Post test drop locations shall be at least 51 mm (2.0 in) away from any BFS depression or other drop impact. Record all measurements on the CTR and determine compliance with drop calibration criteria. Failure to meet clay backing material calibration specifications invalidates the previous six shots. If the backing material meets post test drop specifications, repair the backing material and repeat the pretest drop calibration. If the repaired backing material fixture passes the pretest calibration, it may be reused for the second panel firing sequence, subject to passing another post test drop upon conclusion of the firings.

5.12.4.16   Test Second Armor Panel: Mount the rear panel of the armor sample to a pretest drop calibrated backing material fixture, and repeat the test sequence above using the same test round from section 5.4, table 1 as required for the armor type being tested. Record all results on the CTR.

5.12.4.17   Test Second Armor Sample: Repeat the sequence above for armor sample 2, using the same test round as used for armor sample 1. Record all results on the CTR.

5.12.4.18   Test Third Armor Sample: Replace the backing material fixture with a newly conditioned and drop test calibrated fixture (if necessary). Repeat the test sequence above using test round two from section 5.4, table 1 against armor sample three. Record all results on the CTR.

5.12.4.19 <u>Test Fourth Armor Sample</u>: Repeat the sequence above for armor sample four, using the same test round as used for armor sample three. Record all results in the CTR.

5.12.4.20 <u>Record Results</u>: Record the results of all testing in the CTR (app. A).

5.13 Firing Sequence for Type III Armor

5.13.1 Requirements

(a) One complete armor sample, <u>or</u> two to six primary ballistic panels, plates or inserts, if removable from the armor sample (e.g., front panel protection only).
(b) Six fair hit impacts against each primary ballistic panel, plate(s), or insert(s), a total of 12 impacts per armor sample.
(c) BFS of shot one and the highest remaining velocity shot for each armor panel, plate, or insert.

5.13.2 Acceptance Criteria for Penetration and BFS Compliance

(a) No perforation by the bullet, fragment of the bullet, or fragment from the plate/insert through the armor.
(b) No measured BFS depression depth greater than 44 mm (1.73 in).

5.13.3 Test Range Configuration

Position the front face of the backing material 15 m ± 25 mm (50 ft ± 1.0 in) from the muzzle of the test barrel (fig. 6). Position the velocity measurement instrumentation according to figure 6, item B. Prepare the required test round as specified in section 5.4, table 1. Complete the handload verification requirement (sec. 5.11.2), or fire a sufficient number of pretest rounds (minimum of three) to ensure that the handloaded test round will strike the armor with a velocity within the specified velocity range. Use an appropriate aiming system to ensure proper placement of the test bullet.

5.13.4 Sample Preparation, Mounting, and Firing

5.13.4.1 For armor panels sized and shaped for females, the bust cups shall be filled with backing material conditioned in the same manner as referenced in section 5.7; however, the drop test for consistency does not have to be performed in this area. If the bust cup contains one or more seams, the manufacturer shall submit a detailed diagram to identify the location of each seam, and one shot shall impact a seam.

5.13.4.2 For armor that utilizes a rigid plate or plates such that the armor panel does not make full contact with the backing material surface, the backing material will be built up in a manner that conforms to the armor panel's shape. This buildup will use additional clay backing material conditioned in the same manner as the backing material fixture.

5.13.4.3 Mark the front armor panel, plate, or insert for six impacts, evenly spaced on the panel according to the spacing criteria of a minimum of 76 mm (3.0 in) from any edge to

30

center and 51 mm (2.0 in) from any previous impact (center to center). Wet condition the armor panel, plate, or insert per the requirements of section 5.9.3.

5.13.4.4 Place the exposed surface of the conditioned and drop test calibrated backing material in intimate contact with the backface of the armor panel, plate, or insert and secure it with two vertical and three horizontal elastic straps, 51 mm (2.0 in) wide with Velcro® closures, supplied by the testing laboratory (fig. 8, diagram 1).

5.13.4.5 The straps shall be positioned to leave the strike face impact areas exposed while not permitting the armor to shift on the backing material when impacted. Alternatively, if the strapping is an integral part of the ballistic panel, the manufacturer may supply samples with extended strapping devices to allow the armor as a unit to be mounted on the BMF (fig. 8, diagram 2). The laboratory shall indicate in the CTR which strapping arrangement was used.

5.13.4.6 <u>Firing Sequence</u>: Conduct all six of the firings in accordance with the sequence specified in sections 5.12.4.5 through 5.12.4.14 except for the oblique impacts in items 5.12.4.11, and 5.12.4.12. All shots for Type III armor samples will be at 0° obliquity.

5.13.4.7 <u>Second Panel Testing</u>: Repeat sections 5.13.4.2 through 5.13.4.6 for the second primary ballistic panel, plate, or insert of the sample.

5.13.4.8 <u>Record Test Results</u>: Record the result of all testing in the CTR (app. A).

5.14   Firing Sequence for Type IV Armor

5.14.1 Requirements

(a) One complete armor sample, including at least two primary ballistic panels, plates, or inserts, if removable from complete armor unit (e.g., front panel protection only).
(b) One fair hit impact against the primary ballistic panels, plates, or inserts, a total of two impacts per armor sample.
(c) BFS of each impact.

5.14.2 Acceptance Criteria for Penetration and BFS Compliance

(a) No perforation of the projectile, fragment of the projectile, or fragment of the plate/insert through the armor.
(b) No measured BFS depression depth greater than 44 mm (1.73 in).

5.14.3 Test Range Configuration

Position the front face of the backing material 15 m ± 25 mm (50 ft ± 1.0 in) from the muzzle of the test barrel (fig. 6). Position the velocity measurement instrumentation according to figure 6, item B. Prepare the required test round as specified in section 5.4, table 1. Complete the handload verification requirement (sec. 5.11.2), or fire a sufficient number of pretest rounds (minimum of three) to ensure that the handloaded test round will strike the armor with a velocity within the specified velocity range. Use an appropriate aiming system to ensure proper placement of the test bullet.

5.14.4 Sample Preparation, Mounting, and Firing

5.14.4.1 For armor panels sized and shaped for females, the bust cups shall be filled with backing material conditioned in the same manner as referenced in section 5.7; however, the drop test for consistency does not have to be performed in this area. If the bust cup contains one or more seams, the manufacturer shall submit a detailed diagram to identify the location of each seam, and the shot shall impact a seam.

5.14.4.2 For armor that utilizes a rigid insert, plate or plates such that the armor panel does not make full contact with the backing material surface, the backing material will be built up in a manner that conforms to the armor panel's shape. This buildup will use clay backing material conditioned in the same manner as the backing material fixture.

5.14.4.3 Mark the center of the front armor panel, plate, or insert for one impact, with a minimum of 76 mm (3.0 in) from any edge. Wet condition the armor panel, plate, or insert per the requirements of section 5.9.3.

5.14.4.4 Place the exposed surface of the conditioned and drop test calibrated backing material in intimate contact with the backface of the armor panel, plate, or insert and secure it with at least two vertical and horizontal elastic straps, 51 mm (2.0 in) wide with Velcro® closures, supplied by the testing laboratory (fig. 8, diagram 1).

5.14.4.5 Firing Sequence: Fire one shot at the center of the plate/insert and record the velocity. Examine the plate/insert and the backing material to determine whether the bullet made a fair hit and whether complete penetration occurred. If the bullet failed to make a fair hit as defined by section 3.8, the test must be repeated with another plate/insert sample. If no complete penetration occurred and the bullet made a fair hit, measure the BFS depth of depression using a depth measurement tool. If the depth of the depression complies with the requirement of section 5.14.2, proceed to section 5.14.4.6.

5.14.4.6 Second Plate/Insert Testing: Repeat sections 5.14.4.1 through 5.14.4.5 for the second plate/insert of the sample.

5.14.4.7 Record Test Results: Record the results of all testing in the CTR (app. A).

5.15 P-BFS Test (Special Type)

If the armor is principally made of soft materials (e.g., fabric), use the test procedure defined in section 5.12. If the armor is principally nonfabric, rigid, or "hard" (metal plates or ceramic with a small amount of fabric to act as a trauma shield or to catch backface fragments from the main ballistic resistance element), use the test procedure defined in section 5.13 or 5.14, depending on the NIJ type classification claimed.

5.16 P-BFS Test for Groin and Coccyx Protectors

Groin and coccyx protectors shall each be impacted with three fair hits, evenly spaced not less than 51 mm (2.0 in) apart, and not less than 76 mm (3.0 in) from an edge, at 0° obliquity. The BFS due to the first fair hit shall be measured to determine compliance. No fair hit bullet as defined by section 3.14 shall completely penetrate the armor.

5.17 Baseline Ballistic Limit Determination Test

All NIJ compliance testing for body armor baseline BL assessment will be conducted in accordance with the following procedures.

5.17.1 Types I, IIA, II, and IIIA

Ballistic Limit testing will be completed against complete units (e.g., ballistic fabric panels, covers, carriers, and strapping). Removable trauma inserts/packs will not be included as part of the complete armor unit used for BL determination.

5.17.2 Types III and IV

Testing will be conducted against the complete armor unit as above, except when the armor's NIJ protection type determination and design rely solely upon rigid panels, plates, or inserts to provide ballistic resistance to impact. In those instances, only the rigid panels, plates, or inserts will be tested for baseline BL probability.

5.17.3 Test Sample and Shot Requirements

All NIJ baseline BL testing will be conducted against dry condition armor panels.

Table 2. NIJ baseline Ballistic Limit determination test summary

Armor Samples Required	Ballistic Panels Required	Test Threat	Minimum Shots Required	Minimum Penetration Results
Type I through IIIA One Full Armor	Front	9 mm 124 gr. FMJ	12	5 Complete, 5 Partial, Complete at Highest Velocity
	Rear		12	5 Complete, 5 Partial, Complete at Highest Velocity
Type III One Full Armor	2 - 6*	7.62 mm M80 FMJ	6	3 Complete, 3 Partial, Velocity Range of 27 m/s (90 ft/s)
Type IV One Full Armor	2 - 6*	.30 caliber M2 AP	6	3 Complete, 3 Partial, Velocity Range of 27 m/s (90 ft/s)
Special*	TBD*	TBD*	TBD*	TBD Complete, TBD Partial, Complete at Highest Velocity

*Quantity determined by section 5.17.2 and panel, plate, or insert size and ability to withstand multiple impacts.

5.17.4 Test Range

The ambient conditions and configuration of the test range shall conform to section 5.10 and figure 6 of this document.

5.17.5 Test Rounds

All threat ammunition will be handloaded to achieve the desired velocities.

5.18 Ballistic Limit Testing Equipment

5.18.1 Calibration

All testing equipment shall be calibrated as required by section 5.5.4.

5.18.2 Backing Material Fixture

All NIJ compliance tests for BL testing will use the Backing Material Fixture and Roma Plastilina No. 1 clay backing material as specified in section 4.8, except that the removable wooden back will be removed.

5.18.3 Armor Strapping

The armor panels will be secured to the Backing Material Fixtures in accordance with section 5.11.4.

5.18.4 Test Barrels

All handloaded test rounds will be fired from unvented ANSI/SAAMI velocity test barrels, according to section 5.4.2. All ammunition handling and firing procedures will follow applicable SAAMI specifications and guidelines.

5.18.5 Velocity Measurement

Velocities will be measured in accordance with section 5.5 and figure 6 of this document.

5.19 Ballistic Limit Test Preparation

5.19.1 Shot Location Marking

Types I, IIA, II, and IIIA: The front and rear armor panels will be marked for impact aim points according to figure 9. Types III, IV, and Special: In the case of rigid plates/inserts, the six test round impacts will be evenly distributed over the surface area of the samples according to the spacing criteria in section 3.14.

5.19.2 Sample Conditioning

The armor samples will be conditioned for a minimum of 12 h at the ambient range conditions specified in section 5.10.

5.19.3 Backing Material Conditioning

The backing material fixtures will be prepared and conditioned to the same temperatures as those used to conduct the P-BFS tests for that armor model. Drop test calibration will not be required; however, backing material temperature will be recorded before and after each 12 shot series of firings (one armor panel).

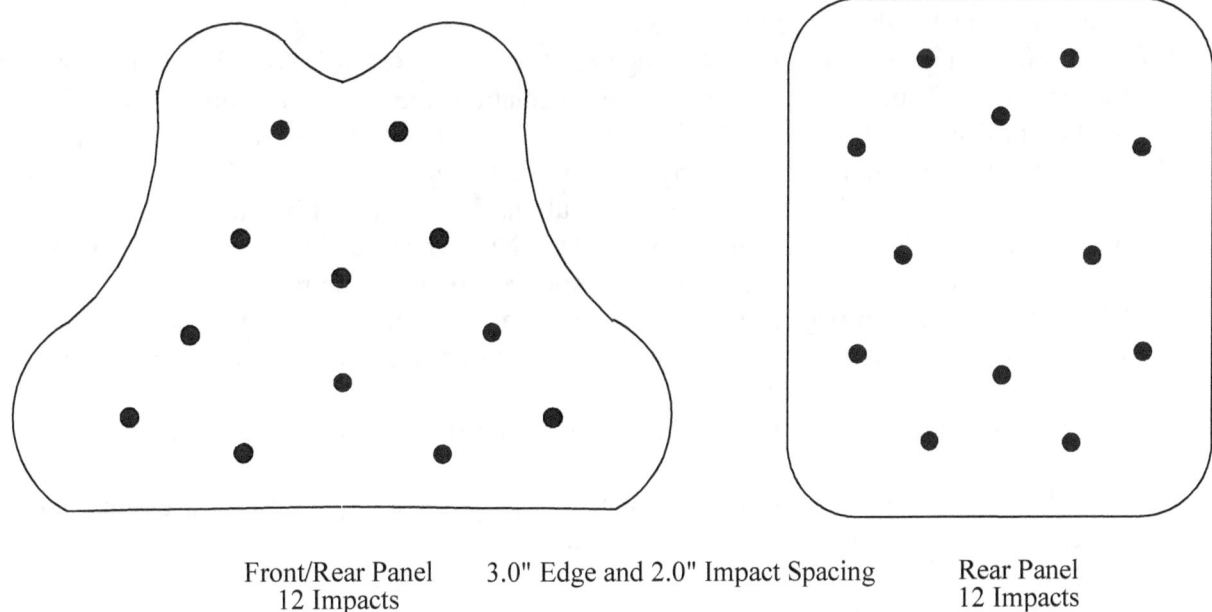

Front/Rear Panel   3.0" Edge and 2.0" Impact Spacing   Rear Panel
12 Impacts   12 Impacts

Figure 9. Impact locations for baseline BL determination testing - Type I through IIIA

5.20 BALLISTIC LIMIT FIRING SEQUENCE

ALL BALLISTIC LIMIT DETERMINATION TESTING FOR NIJ COMPLIANCE ARMORS WILL FOLLOW THE GENERAL GUIDELINES AND PROCEDURES OF MIL–STD–662F AND TOP 2–2–710 WITH INCLUSION AND ADHERENCE TO THE FOLLOWING MODIFICATIONS:

(a) All Type I through IIIA test samples will be tested in their final design and end use configuration, including all system components (e.g., carriers, straps), with the exception of trauma inserts/packs, which will be removed. Type III and IV test samples will be tested according to the relevant requirements of section 5.17.2, determined by NIJ CTP personnel upon receipt of the armor for compliance testing.

(b) Impact locations for all shots will be permanently marked on the armor panel impact face according to the pattern requirements of figure 9 and section 5.19.1.

(c) The minimum aim point spacing between the edges of the ballistic panel insert, not the external carrier, will be 76 mm (3.0 in), and the minimum spacing between each impact will be 51 mm (2.0 in).

(d) The armor panel shall be rigidly supported across the entire rear face area by the backing material fixture specified in section 4.8 of this document, except that the removable wooden back shall be removed from the backing material fixture.

(e) The armor panel shall be positioned and maintained in intimate contact with the backing material prior to and during the impact event, using the strapping devices specified in section 5.11.4 and figure 8 of this document.

(f) The armor panel will be adjusted between shots as required to maintain a consistent armor panel surface, original condition, alignment of the ballistic panels/layers, and intimate contact with the backing material.

(g) A modified Langlie Method of test firing (TOP 2–2–710, Ref. [6]) will be used to acquire the data set for Types I, IIA, II, and IIIA BL evaluations (app. B). The "up and down" method of firing (MIL–STD–662F, Ref. [5]) will be utilized for Types III and IV testing.

(h) The lower velocity limit for beginning the modified Langlie sequence will be supplied to the laboratory by the NIJ CTP as part of the submission request. If the lower velocity is not provided, the lower limit will be the model's NIJ Type reference velocity plus 69 m/s (225 ft/s). The lower velocity limit should produce a partial penetration.

(i) The upper velocity for beginning the modified Langlie firing sequence will be the lower velocity limit plus 46 m/s (150 ft/s). This may be adjusted as needed during testing to ensure meeting steps j and k below.

(j) The highest velocity impact obtained during the modified Langlie test sequence must be a complete penetration.

(k) If the highest velocity fired during the modified Langlie test sequence produces a partial penetration, firing will continue at 15 m/s (50 ft/s) increments until a single complete penetration is achieved.

5.21   Ballistic Limit Determination

5.21.1 Minimum Number of Data Points

a) <u>Levels I, IIA, II, and IIIA</u>: A minimum of 12 data points are required, including at least five partial and five complete penetration results.
b) <u>Levels III and IV</u>: A minimum of six data points are required, consisting of three partial and three complete penetration results.
c) <u>Special</u>: The minimum number of data points will be determined by user specification and NIJ approval, and shall require an equal number of partial and complete penetrations for the BL calculation.

5.21.2 Data Set Tabulation

The data set will be tabulated and sorted according to velocity and penetration results. The sorted data must include the lowest complete penetration (CP) velocity result and the highest partial penetration (PP) velocity result.

5.21.3 Ballistic Limit Calculation

<u>Levels I, IIA, II, and IIIA</u>: The arithmetic mean of 10 qualified (5 CP, 5 PP) velocities is calculated, producing the armor panel's 10 shot baseline BL. The standard deviation (σ) of the 10 shot group of velocities will also be determined and recorded along with the model's baseline BL in the CTR.

<u>Levels III and IV</u>: The arithmetic mean of six qualified (3 CP, 3 PP) velocities is calculated, producing the armor sample's six shot baseline BL. The standard deviation (σ) of the six shot group of velocities will also be determined and recorded along with the model's baseline BL in the CTR.

<u>Special</u>: The arithmetic mean of either six or 10 qualified velocities is calculated, producing the armor panel's six or 10 shot baseline BL. The standard deviation (σ) of the six or 10 shot group of velocities will also be determined and recorded along with the model's baseline BL in the CTR.

5.22 Ballistic Limit Retesting of Compliant Armor

When compliant body armor models are submitted to NIJ for BL retest, two complete sets or samples will be required according to section 4.7, section 5.17.2, and table 2. The samples will be the same size as originally submitted. The BL and standard deviation of each sample/panel from one of the retest armor samples will be determined in accordance with sections 5.17 through 5.21. The remaining armor sample will be retained for use as needed, should the armor sample fail to meet the retest criteria.

Retested armor will continue to be compliant if the BL of the retested sample is ± 3 σ from each of the baseline BL determined during its original compliance testing. Armor found noncompliant with its baseline BL will undergo additional discretionary investigation by the NIJ

CTP. Compliance determinations using NIJ Standard–0101.04 BL procedures and retest criteria apply to new, unworn, manufacturer supplied body armor samples only.

6. DATA COLLECTION AND REPORTING

6.1   Test Documentation

6.1.1   Data Recording

The results of each armor test performed will be recorded on the CTR (app. A). All test data and activities shall be recorded in sufficient detail such that a reconstruction of the test based on the information contained in the CTR can be performed.

6.1.2   Data Certification

When completed, the responsible test laboratory representative shall sign the CTR and any attachments.

6.1.3   Data Storage

All CTRs and accompanying data will be archived, in either digital or hardcopy form, by the test laboratory for a minimum of five years following the completion of each compliance test series.

6.2   Test Report

6.2.1   Requirements

A summary report will be submitted to the NIJ CTP Office within 10 working days of the completion of testing. Inclusion of the following minimum support documentations will be required:

(a) Submission letter stating the outcome of the testing.
(b) Compliance Test Report (signed).
(c) Failure documentation (if applicable).
(d) At least one photograph showing the strike face(s) of a representative armor sample (e.g., front and back) before testing, with scale and identification sign.
(e) At least one photograph showing the strike face(s) of the tested armor sample (e.g., front and back panels), with scale and identification sign.

APPENDIX A

COMPLIANCE TEST REPORT FORM

The Compliance Test Report (CTR) form shall be used in conjunction with NIJ Standard–0101.04, <u>Ballistic Resistance of Personal Body Armor</u>, and shall become a part of the official records of the compliance testing of each armor model submitted for testing. All sections of the form shall be completed.

An electronic file of this report form is available from the NIJ Compliance Test Program Office, National Law Enforcement and Corrections Technology Center - National (NLECTC-National). Requests for this file can be sent to, NLECTC-National, NIJ Body Armor Compliance Test Program, P.O. Box 1160, Rockville, MD 20849–1160, Attn: Compliance Test Program Manager, or to: E-mail: <u>asknlectc@nlectc.org</u>.

COMPLIANCE TESTING INFORMATION

FACILITY DESCRIPTION:

Test Laboratory: _____
Test Start Date: _____

Report Number: _____
Report Date: _____

ARMOR DESCRIPTION:

Manufacturer: _____
Date Rec'd: _____
*Ballistic Material: _____

Model: _____
Style: _____
Male/Female: _____

NIJ Armor Type: _____
0101.03 Compliant: _____

*Choices:	Aramid	PBO	Ceramic	Metal
	Polyethylene	Hybrid	Composite	Other

SAMPLE DESCRIPTION:

	Sample 1		Sample 2		Sample 3		Sample 4		Sample 5	
	Front	Back	Front	Back	Front	Back	Front	Back	Front	Back
Size:										
Serial Number:										
Lot Number:										
Gross Weight (lb.):										

TEST DESCRIPTION:

	P-BFS								BL (V50)	
	Sample 1		Sample 2		Sample 3		Sample 4		Sample 5	
	Front	Back	Front	Back	Front	Back	Front	Back	Front	Back
Test Condition:	Wet	Wet	Wet	Wet	Wet	Wet	Wet	Wet	Dry	Dry
Threat Ammunition:		0	0	0		0	0	0		0
Reference Vo (± 30 ft/s):		0	0	0		0	0	0		0
Bullet (grain/type):		0	0	0		0	0	0		0
Bullet Manufacturer:		0	0	0		0	0	0		0
Factory Lot Number:		0	0	0		0	0	0		0
Barrel Manufacturer:		0	0	0		0	0	0		0
Caliber:		0	0	0		0	0	0		0
Length (in):		0.0	0.0	0.0		0.0	0.0	0.0		0.0
Receiver:		0	0	0	0	0	0	0	0	0

Starting Vo for BL (provided)

ARMOR CONSTRUCTION:

Front Panel   Rear Panel

Front Closure (Y/N): _____

Removable Carrier (Y/N): _____   _____

Number of Layers: _____   _____

Description of Stitching: _____   _____
_____   _____

Individual Layer Description: _____   _____
_____   _____

REMARKS:
_____
_____
_____

TESTING CERTIFICATION:

Laboratory Representative: _____
Name

Witnessed by: _____
Name   Representing

_____
Signature

_____
Signature

NATIONAL INSTITUTE OF JUSTICE
COMPLIANCE TEST REPORT

Daily Wet Conditioning Spray Calibration

Report Number: 0
Report Date: 01/00/00

Manufacturer: 0
Model: 0

Calibration Date:

Gauge Location	15	15	15	Interval (min) 15	15	15	15	
1								inches
2								inches
3								inches
4								inches
5								inches

Average:	#DIV/0!	#DIV/0!	#DIV/0!	#DIV/0!	#DIV/0!	#DIV/0!	inches
Requirement:	*1.0*	*1.0*	*1.0*	*1.0*	*1.0*	*1.0*	*inches*
Pass:	**#DIV/0!**	**#DIV/0!**	**#DIV/0!**	**#DIV/0!**	**#DIV/0!**	**#DIV/0!**	

Required Flow Rate: 4.0 +/- 0.8 in/hr   1.0 +/- 0.2 in/.25 hr

Conditioning Surface Dimensions: ____ x ____ ____ inches square

Gauge Locations

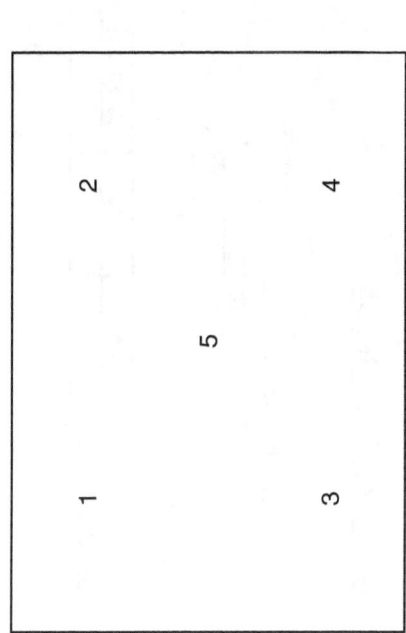

1   2

5

3   4

Top View

Spray Condition Cal

NATIONAL INSTITUTE OF JUSTICE
COMPLIANCE TEST REPORT

Drop Test Results

Report Number: 0
Report Date: 01/00/00

Sample/Panel: Sample 1 Front
Manufacturer: 0
Model: 0

Test Date: _____
Range Conditions:
Temperature: _____ F
RH: _____ %

Pre-Test Drop Calibration:

Block ID: _____
Time of Day: _____ hrs
Clay Temperature: _____ deg. F

Depth of Indent:	Drop 1	Drop 2	Drop 3	Drop 4	Drop 5	Avg.
						#DIV/0!

Requirement: 20 ± 3
Pass: #DIV/0!

Post-Test Drop Calibration:

Block ID: 0
Time of Day: _____ hrs
Clay Temperature: _____ deg. F

Depth of Indent:	Drop 1	Drop 2	Drop 3	Drop 4	Drop 5	Avg.
						#DIV/0!

Requirement: 20 ± 3
Pass: #DIV/0!

Report Number: 0
Report Date: 01/00/00

Sample/Panel: Sample 1 Back

Test Date: 01/00/00
Range Conditions:
Temperature: 0 F
RH: 0 %

Pre-Test Drop Calibration:

Block ID: _____
Time of Day: _____ hrs
Clay Temperature: _____ deg. F

Depth of Indent:	Drop 1	Drop 2	Drop 3	Drop 4	Drop 5	Avg.
						#DIV/0!

Requirement: 20 ± 3
Pass: #DIV/0!

Post-Test Drop Calibration:

Block ID: 0
Time of Day: _____ hrs
Clay Temperature: _____ deg. F

Depth of Indent:	Drop 1	Drop 2	Drop 3	Drop 4	Drop 5	Avg.
						#DIV/0!

Requirement: 20 ± 3
Pass: #DIV/0!

Drop Test Results

Report Number: 0
Report Date: 01/00/00

Sample/Panel: Sample 2 Front
Manufacturer: 0
Model: 0

Test Date:
Range Conditions:
Temperature: _____ F
RH: _____ %

Pre-Test Drop Calibration:

Block ID:
Time of Day: _____ hrs
Clay Temperature: _____ deg. F

Depth of Indent:	Drop 1	Drop 2	Drop 3	Drop 4	Drop 5	Avg.
						#DIV/0!

Requirement: 20 ± 3
Pass: #DIV/0!

Post-Test Drop Calibration:

Block ID: 0
Time of Day: _____ hrs
Clay Temperature: _____ deg. F

Depth of Indent:	Drop 1	Drop 2	Drop 3	Drop 4	Drop 5	Avg.
						#DIV/0!

Requirement: 20 ± 3
Pass: #DIV/0!

Report Number: 0
Report Date: 01/00/00

Sample/Panel: Sample 2 Back

Test Date: 01/00/00
Range Conditions:
Temperature: 0 F
RH: 0 %

Pre-Test Drop Calibration:

Block ID:
Time of Day: _____ hrs
Clay Temperature: _____ deg. F

Depth of Indent:	Drop 1	Drop 2	Drop 3	Drop 4	Drop 5	Avg.
						#DIV/0!

Requirement: 20 ± 3
Pass: #DIV/0!

Post-Test Drop Calibration:

Block ID: 0
Time of Day: _____ hrs
Clay Temperature: _____ deg. F

Depth of Indent:	Drop 1	Drop 2	Drop 3	Drop 4	Drop 5	Avg.
						#DIV/0!

Requirement: 20 ± 3
Pass: #DIV/0!

NATIONAL INSTITUTE OF JUSTICE
COMPLIANCE TEST REPORT

Drop Test Results

Report Number: 0
Report Date: 01/00/00

Sample/Panel: Sample 3   Front
Manufacturer: 0
Model: 0

Test Date: _____
Range Conditions:
Temperature: ____ F
RH: ____ %

Pre-Test Drop Calibration:

Block ID: _____
Time of Day: _____ hrs
Clay Temperature: _____ deg. F

Depth of Indent:	Drop 1	Drop 2	Drop 3	Drop 4	Drop 5	Avg.
						#DIV/0!

Requirement: 20 ± 3
Pass: #DIV/0!

Post-Test Drop Calibration:

Block ID: 0
Time of Day: _____ hrs
Clay Temperature: _____ deg. F

Depth of Indent:	Drop 1	Drop 2	Drop 3	Drop 4	Drop 5	Avg.
						#DIV/0!

Requirement: 20 ± 3
Pass: #DIV/0!

Report Number: 0
Report Date: 01/00/00

Sample/Panel: Sample 3   Back

Test Date: 01/00/00
Range Conditions:
Temperature: 0 F
RH: 0 %

Pre-Test Drop Calibration:

Block ID: _____
Time of Day: _____ hrs
Clay Temperature: _____ deg. F

Depth of Indent:	Drop 1	Drop 2	Drop 3	Drop 4	Drop 5	Avg.
						#DIV/0!

Requirement: 20 ± 3
Pass: #DIV/0!

Post-Test Drop Calibration:

Block ID: 0
Time of Day: _____ hrs
Clay Temperature: _____ deg. F

Depth of Indent:	Drop 1	Drop 2	Drop 3	Drop 4	Drop 5	Avg.
						#DIV/0!

Requirement: 20 ± 3
Pass: #DIV/0!

NATIONAL INSTITUTE OF JUSTICE
COMPLIANCE TEST REPORT

Report Number: 0
Report Date: 01/00/00

Drop Test Results

Sample/Panel: Sample 4   Front
Manufacturer: 0
Model: 0

Test Date:
Range Conditions:
Temperature: _____ F
RH: _____ %

Pre-Test Drop Calibration:

Block ID:
Time of Day: _____ hrs
Clay Temperature: _____ deg. F

	Drop 1	Drop 2	Drop 3	Drop 4	Drop 5	Avg.
Depth of Indent:						#DIV/0!
				Requirement:		20 ± 3
				Pass:		#DIV/0!

Post-Test Drop Calibration:

Block ID: 0
Time of Day: _____ hrs
Clay Temperature: _____ deg. F

	Drop 1	Drop 2	Drop 3	Drop 4	Drop 5	Avg.
Depth of Indent:						#DIV/0!
				Requirement:		20 ± 3
				Pass:		#DIV/0!

Sample/Panel: Sample 4   Back

Report Number: 0
Report Date: 01/00/00

Test Date: 01/00/00
Range Conditions:
Temperature: 0 F
RH: 0 %

Pre-Test Drop Calibration:

Block ID:
Time of Day: _____ hrs
Clay Temperature: _____ deg. F

	Drop 1	Drop 2	Drop 3	Drop 4	Drop 5	Avg.
Depth of Indent:						#DIV/0!
				Requirement:		20 ± 3
				Pass:		#DIV/0!

Post-Test Drop Calibration:

Block ID: 0
Time of Day: _____ hrs
Clay Temperature: _____ deg. F

	Drop 1	Drop 2	Drop 3	Drop 4	Drop 5	Avg.
Depth of Indent:						#DIV/0!
				Requirement:		20 ± 3
				Pass:		#DIV/0!

NATIONAL INSTITUTE OF JUSTICE
COMPLIANCE TEST REPORT

Penetration and BFS Firing Data

Sample No: Sample 1	**Ammunition:** 0
Manufacturer: 0	**Conditioning:** Wet
Model: 0	**Test Date:** 01/00/00

Report Number: 0	
Report Date: 01/00/00	
NIJ Armor Type: 0	

Panel Serial No: 0

Panel Serial No: 0

FRONT PANEL

Shot No.	Velocity (m/s)	Velocity (ft/s)	Fair (Y/N)	Penetrate (Y/N)	Remarks	BFS (mm)
1						
2						
3						
4						
5						
6						
7						
8						

BACK PANEL

Shot No.	Velocity (m/s)	Velocity (ft/s)	Fair (Y/N)	Penetrate (Y/N)	Remarks	BFS (mm)
1						
2						
3						
4						
5						
6						
7						
8						

COMPLIANCE

Front Panel	Back Panel

Firing Sequence Start: _____ hrs
Firing Sequence End: _____ hrs
Duration: _____ min

Firing Sequence Start: _____ hrs
Firing Sequence End: _____ hrs
Duration: _____ min

TEST CONDITIONS:
Ambient Temp: 0.0 F
Rel. Humidity: 0.0 %

TEST RANGE:
Range Length: _____ m
_____ ft.

Handload Verification: _____ ft/s

Reference Velocity: 0 ft/s

Velocity Range: -30 / 30 ft/s

Velocity Results:	Min	Max	
Front Panel:	0	0	ft/s
Back Panel:	0	0	ft/s

REMARKS:
a - 30 degree obliquity impact
b - Excessive velocity
c - Insufficient velocity
d - Too close to edge
e - Too close to prior impact
f - Excessive total impacts (test terminated)
g - Excessive area impacts (test terminated)
h - Impact on seam

NATIONAL INSTITUTE OF JUSTICE
COMPLIANCE TEST REPORT

Penetration and BFS Firing Data

Sample No:	Sample 2
Manufacturer:	0
Model:	0

Ammunition:	0
Conditioning:	Wet
Test Date:	01/00/00

Report Number:	0
Report Date:	01/00/00
NIJ Armor Type:	0

Panel Serial No: 0

Panel Serial No: 0

FRONT PANEL

Shot No.	Velocity (m/s)	Velocity (ft/s)	Fair (Y/N)	Penetrate (Y/N)	Remarks	BFS (mm)
1						
2						
3						
4						
5						
6						
7						
8						

Firing Sequence Start:		hrs
Firing Sequence End:		hrs
Duration:		min

BACK PANEL

Shot No.	Velocity (m/s)	Velocity (ft/s)	Fair (Y/N)	Penetrate (Y/N)	Remarks	BFS (mm)
1						
2						
3						
4						
5						
6						
7						
8						

Firing Sequence Start:		hrs
Firing Sequence End:		hrs
Duration:		min

COMPLIANCE

Front Panel	Back Panel

TEST CONDITIONS:

| Ambient Temp: | 0.0 | F |
| Rel. Humidity: | 0.0 | % |

TEST RANGE:

| Range Length: | 0.0 | m |
| | 0.0 | ft. |

Handload Verification:		ft/s
Reference Velocity:	0	ft/s
Velocity Range:	-30	30	ft/s

Velocity Results:	Min	Max	
Front Panel:	0	0	ft/s
Back Panel:	0	0	ft/s

REMARKS:

a - 30 degree obliquity impact
b - Excessive velocity
c - Insufficient velocity
d - Too close to edge
e - Too close to prior impact
f - Excessive total impacts (test terminated)
g - Excessive area impacts (test terminated)
h - Impact on seam

NATIONAL INSTITUTE OF JUSTICE
COMPLIANCE TEST REPORT

Penetration and BFS Firing Data

Sample No: Sample 3
Manufacturer: 0
Model: 0

Ammunition: 0
Conditioning: Wet
Test Date: 01/00/00

Report Number: 0
Report Date: 01/00/00
NIJ Armor Type: 0

Panel Serial No: 0

Panel Serial No: 0

FRONT PANEL

Shot No.	Velocity (m/s)	Velocity (ft/s)	Fair (Y/N)	Penetrate (Y/N)	Remarks	BFS (mm)
1						
2						
3						
4						
5						
6						
7						
8						

Firing Sequence Start: _____ hrs
Firing Sequence End: _____ hrs
Duration: _____ min

BACK PANEL

Shot No.	Velocity (m/s)	Velocity (ft/s)	Fair (Y/N)	Penetrate (Y/N)	Remarks	BFS (mm)
1						
2						
3						
4						
5						
6						
7						
8						

Firing Sequence Start: _____ hrs
Firing Sequence End: _____ hrs
Duration: _____ min

COMPLIANCE	
Front Panel	Back Panel

TEST CONDITIONS:
Ambient Temp: 0 F
Rel. Humidity: 0 %

TEST RANGE:
Range Length: _____ m
_____ ft.

Handload Verification: _____ ft/s

Reference Velocity: 0 _____ ft/s

Velocity Range: -30 30 ft/s

Velocity Results:	Min	Max
Front Panel:	0	0
Back Panel:	0	0
	ft/s	ft/s

REMARKS:
a - 30 degree obliquity impact
b - Excessive velocity
c - Insufficient velocity
d - Too close to edge
e - Too close to prior impact
f - Excessive total impacts (test terminated)
g - Excessive area impacts (test terminated)
h - Impact on seam

NATIONAL INSTITUTE OF JUSTICE
COMPLIANCE TEST REPORT

Penetration and BFS Firing Data

Sample No: Sample 4
Manufacturer: 0
Model: 0

Report Number: 0
Report Date: 01/00/00
NIJ Armor Type: 0

Ammunition: 0
Conditioning: Wet
Test Date: 01/00/00

Panel Serial No: 0

Panel Serial No: 0

FRONT PANEL

Shot No.	Velocity (m/s)	Velocity (ft/s)	Fair (Y/N)	Penetrate (Y/N)	Remarks	BFS (mm)
1						
2						
3						
4						
5						
6						
7						
8						

Firing Sequence Start: _____ hrs
Firing Sequence End: _____ hrs
Duration: _____ min

BACK PANEL

Shot No.	Velocity (m/s)	Velocity (ft/s)	Fair (Y/N)	Penetrate (Y/N)	Remarks	BFS (mm)
1						
2						
3						
4						
5						
6						
7						
8						

Firing Sequence Start: _____ hrs
Firing Sequence End: _____ hrs
Duration: _____ min

COMPLIANCE

Front Panel	Back Panel

TEST CONDITIONS:
Ambient Temp: _0_ F
Rel. Humidity: _0_ %

TEST RANGE:
Range Length: _0.0_ m
_0.0_ ft.

Handload Verification: _____ ft/s

Reference Velocity: _0_ ft/s

Velocity Range: -30 to 30 ft/s

Velocity Results:

	Min	Max
Front Panel:	0	0
Back Panel:	0	0

REMARKS:
a - 30 degree obliquity impact
b - Excessive velocity
c - Insufficient velocity
d - Too close to edge
e - Too close to prior impact
f - Excessive total impacts (test terminated)
g - Excessive area impacts (test terminated)
h - Impact on seam

NATIONAL INSTITUTE OF JUSTICE
COMPLIANCE TEST REPORT

Ballistic Limit Firing Data

Sample No: Sample 5
Manufacturer: 0
Model: 0

Serial No: 0
Weight: 0 _____ lb.

Ammunition: 0
Conditioning: Dry
Test Date: _____

Report Number: 0
Report Date: 01/00/00
NIJ Armor Type: 0

Serial No: 0
Weight: 0.00 _____ lb.

FRONT PANEL

Shot No.	Velocity (m/s)	Velocity (ft/s)	Shot Result Complete	Shot Result Partial	Remarks	Used (Y/N)
1						
9						
7						
6						
12						
5						
3						
4						
10						
11						
8						
2						
13						
14						
15						
Total:	0	0	0	0		0

BACK PANEL

Shot No.	Velocity (m/s)	Velocity (ft/s)	Shot Result Complete	Shot Result Partial	Remarks	Used (Y/N)
1						
7						
6						
8						
9						
12						
5						
4						
10						
2						
11						
3						
13						
14						
15						
Total:	0	0	0	0		0

TEST RANGE:

Range Length: 0.0 m
0.0 ft.

TEST CONDITIONS:
Ambient Temp: _____ F
Rel. Humidity: _____ %

REMARKS:
a - Too close to edge
b - Too close to prior impact
c - Impact on seam

NIJ Reference Velocity: _____ ft/s
NIJ Calculated Start Velocity: 0 ft/s
Provided Start Velocity: 0 ft/s
Upper Velocity: 150 ft/s

Velocity Results:	Min	Max	
Front Panel:	0	0	ft/s
Back Panel:	0	0	ft/s

NATIONAL INSTITUTE OF JUSTICE
COMPLIANCE TEST REPORT

Report Number: 0
Report Date: 0
NIJ Armor Type: 0

Ballistic Limit Firing Data Sheet

Sample No: Sample 5
Manufacturer: 0
Model: 0

Panel Serial No: 0

Ammunition: 0
Conditioning: Dry
Test Date: #####

Panel Serial No: 0

10 - SHOT BALLISTIC LIMIT - TYPE I, IIA, II, IIIA

| FRONT PANEL | | Shot Result | | BACK PANEL | | | Shot Result | |
Shot No.	Velocity (m/s)	Velocity (ft/s)	Complete	Partial	Shot No.	Velocity (m/s)	Velocity (ft/s)	Complete	Partial

NIJ BASELINE BL:

Front:	#DIV/0!	ft/s
Vo Range:	0	ft/s
Std Dev. (σ)	#DIV/0!	ft/s
Back:	#DIV/0!	ft/s
Vo Range:	0	ft/s
Std Dev. (σ)	#DIV/0!	ft/s
Difference F-to-B:	#DIV/0!	ft/s
Avg. F-to-B 6-shot V50:	#DIV/0!	ft/s

6 - SHOT BALLISTIC LIMIT - TYPE III, IV

| FRONT PANEL | | Shot Result | | BACK PANEL | | | Shot Result | |
Shot No.	Velocity (m/s)	Velocity (ft/s)	Complete	Partial	Shot No.	Velocity (m/s)	Velocity (ft/s)	Complete	Partial

NIJ BASELINE BL:

Front:	#DIV/0!	ft/s
Vo Range:	0	ft/s
Std Dev. (σ)	#DIV/0!	ft/s
Back:	#DIV/0!	ft/s
Vo Range:	0	ft/s
Std Dev. (σ)	#DIV/0!	ft/s
Difference F-to-B:	#DIV/0!	ft/s
Avg. F-to-B 6-shot V50:	#DIV/0!	ft/s

NATIONAL INSTITUTE OF JUSTICE
COMPLIANCE TEST REPORT

Summary of Results

Armor Manufacturer: 0 _____
Armor Model No: 0 _____

Armor Style: 0 _____
NIJ Armor Type: 0 _____

Report Number: 0
Report Date: 01/00/00

PENETRATION AND BACKFACE SIGNATURE

Item Number	Test Samples (b) Serial Number	Panel	Weight (lbs)	No. of Plies	Caliber (a)	Ballistic Threat Obliquity (degrees)	Req'd Shots	Velocity (ft/s) Max.	Velocity (ft/s) Min.	Penetration (Y/N)	Results (a) Deformation (mm) Shot 1	Results (a) Deformation (mm) Shot 2
Sample 1	0	Front	0	0	0	0	4	0	0	N	0	0
	0	Back	0	0	0	30	2	0	0	N	0	0
Sample 2	0	Front	0	0	0	0	4	0	0	N	0	0
	0	Back	0	0	0	30	2	0	0	N	0	0
Sample 3	0	Front	0	0	0	0	4	0	0	N	0	0
	0	Back	0	0	0	30	2	0	0	N	0	0
Sample 4	0	Front	0	0	0	0	4	0	0	N	0	0
	0	Back	0	0	0	30	2	0	0	N	0	0

Notes:
(a) Maximum allowable BFS: 44 mm
(b) Ballistic Material: 0

P-BFS Compliance:
Penetration: Pass
BFS: Pass

NIJ Baseline BL:
Front Panel: #DIV/0! ft/s
Std Dev. (σ): #DIV/0! ft/s
Rear Panel: #DIV/0! ft/s
Std Dev. (σ): #DIV/0! ft/s

CERTIFICATION:

Test Data Certification: 0

_____ Name

_____ Signature

Witnessed by: 0

_____ 0 _____
Name   Representing

_____ Signature

APPENDIX B

MODIFIED
LANGLIE METHOD OF BALLISTIC LIMIT FIRING

1. VELOCITY CLASS DETERMINATION

1.1 Velocity Limits

Select a lower and upper projectile velocity limit so that the probability of obtaining a complete penetration at the lower velocity or a partial penetration at the upper velocity is highly unlikely.

(a) The lower velocity should be provided by NIJ or the manufacturer — if not, the lower velocity limit shall be the highest of the two NIJ Standard–0101.04 Type ammunition reference velocities plus 69 m/s (225 ft/s).
(b) The upper velocity will be determined by adding 46 m/s (150 ft/s) to the lower velocity limit.

2. PROCEDURE

2.1 Firing Sequence

(a) Attempt to fire the first round at a velocity midway between the lower and upper limit velocities.
(b) If no upper limit is known, attempt to fire the first round at a velocity 46 m/s (150 ft/s) above the lower limit.
(c) If the first round results in a complete penetration, attempt to reduce the velocity of the second round halfway between the first round velocity and the lower limit velocity; if the first round results in a partial penetration, attempt to raise the velocity of the second round halfway between the first and upper limit velocity.
(d) If the first two rounds result in a reversal (one partial, one complete penetration), attempt to fire the third round halfway between the velocity of the first two rounds.
(e) If the first two rounds result in two partial penetrations, attempt to fire the third round at a velocity halfway between the second round velocity and the upper velocity limit.
(f) If the first two rounds result in two complete penetrations, attempt to fire the third round halfway between the second round velocity and the lower velocity limit.

Fire the remaining rounds using the following rules:

(g) If the preceding pair of rounds resulted in a reversal (one partial, one complete penetration), attempt to fire at a velocity halfway between the two velocities.

(h) If the last two rounds did not produce a reversal, look at the last four rounds. If the number of partial and complete penetrations is equal, attempt to fire the next round halfway between the velocity of the first and last round of the group.

(i) If the last four rounds did not produce an equal number of partial and complete penetrations, look at the last six, eight, etc., until the number of partial and complete penetrations are equal. Attempt to fire the next round halfway between the lower and upper velocities of that group.

(j) Always attempt to fire at a velocity halfway between the lower and upper velocity of the group examined.

(k) If the conditions of section 1.1 cannot be satisfied and the last round fired resulted in a complete penetration, attempt to fire the next round at a velocity halfway between the last round and the lower velocity limit; otherwise, if the last round was a partial penetration, attempt to fire halfway between the last round and the upper velocity limit.

(l) Continue on in the manner above until the requirement for the number of rounds has been satisfied, i.e., a minimum of 12 rounds, with at least five partial and five complete penetrations, with the highest velocity round resulting in a complete penetration.

2.2   Velocity Class Adjustment

In cases where it becomes rapidly obvious that the lower velocity limit is too high or too low, adjustment of the velocity classes can be made by selecting a new lower velocity limit and adjusting the upper limit to be 46 m/s (150 ft/s) higher than the new lower limit.

APPENDIX C

BODY ARMOR SELECTION

Police administrators should make every effort to encourage their officers to wear body armor throughout each duty shift. Although designed primarily to provide protection against handgun assault, body armor has prevented serious and potentially fatal injuries in traffic accidents (both in automobiles and while operating motorcycles), from physical assault with improvised clubs, and to some extent from knives. Law enforcement officer fatality statistics are compiled annually by the Federal Bureau of Investigation. Analysis of the statistics suggests that a large percentage of the officer fatalities reported each year could have been prevented if the officer had been wearing armor. Before purchasing body armor one should read NIJ Guide 100 –98, "Selection and Application Guide to Personal Body Armor," which discusses armor in depth.

The fundamental considerations in selecting body armor are the threat to which officers are exposed and the nature of their service weapons. Knowledge of the street weapons in the local area (confiscated weapons are a good indicator) is essential, for the armor should be selected to protect against the street threat and the department's service weapons. Throughout the last decade, one in six officers killed with a firearm was shot with his or her duty weapon. Full coverage of the torso is critical because fatalities among officers wearing body armor have resulted from bullets having entered an officer's side through the opening between front and rear panels. NIJ Standard–0101.04 classifies body armor into seven different threat levels that, in order from lowest to highest level of protection, are Type I, Type IIA, Type II, Type IIIA, Type III, Type IV, and Special.

As of the year 2000, ballistic resistant body armor suitable for full time wear throughout an entire shift of duty is available in classification Types I, IIA, II, and IIIA, which provide increasing levels of protection from handgun threats. Type I body armor, which was first issued during the NIJ demonstration project in 1975, is the minimum level of protection that any officer should have. Officers seeking protection from lower velocity 9 mm and 40 S&W ammunition should wear Type IIA body armor. For protection against high velocity 357 Magnum and higher velocity 9 mm ammunition, officers traditionally select Type II body armor. Type IIIA body armor provides the highest level of protection available in concealable body armor and provides protection from high velocity 9 mm and 44 Magnum ammunition.

As noted above, while 100 % protection in all circumstances is impossible, the routine use of appropriate body armor significantly reduces the likelihood of fatal injury. Body armor selection is to some extent a tradeoff between ballistic protection and wearability. The weight and bulk of body armor are inversely proportional to the level of ballistic protection it provides; therefore, comfort decreases as the protection level increases. All departments should strive to select body armor that their officers will wear, consistent with their ballistic protection requirements. Agencies should ensure that each officer knows and understands the protection that it affords, as well as its limitations. Body armor that is not worn provides *no* protection.

APPENDIX D

ACCEPTABLE BULLETS FOR HANDLOADING

All jacket materials shall be of copper or copper alloy (approximately 90 % copper and 10 % zinc). No steel, brass, or other jacket material is permitted.

Totally Enclosed Metal Case (TEMC), Total Metal Jacket (TMJ), Total Metal Case (TMC), and any other nomenclature for electro-deposited copper or cupro-nickel jackets are acceptable for use in testing when FMJ is specified.

THREAT LEVEL	CALIBER	BULLET WT. (g/gr.)	BULLET DESCRIPTION	BULLET DIA. (nominal)
	22 LR*	2.6/40	LRN	5.6 mm (.222 in)
I	380 ACP	6.2/95	FMJ RN	9 mm (.355 in)
IIA	9 mm	8.0/124	FMJ RN	9 mm (.355 in)
	40 S&W	11.7/180	FMJ	10 mm (.400 in)
II	9 mm	8.0/124	FMJ RN	9 mm (.355 in)
	357 Mag	10.2/158	JSP	9.1 mm (.357 in)
IIIA	9 mm	8.0/124	FMJ RN	9 mm (.355 in)
	44 Mag	15.6/240	JHP	10.9 mm (.429 in)
III	7.62 mm NATO	9.6/147	FMJ- SPIRE PT BT**	7.62 mm (.308 in)
IV	30.06 M2 AP	10.8/166	FMJ – SPIRE PT AP***	7.62 mm (.308 in)

* Commercially loaded ammunition may be used—handloading of this round is not required. See section 5.4.1.
** Verify that jacket and/or core is nonferrous (use of a magnet is acceptable).
*** Obtained from U.S. Military M2 AP ammunition.

U.S. Department of Justice
Office of Justice Programs
810 Seventh Street N.W.
Washington, DC 20531

Janet Reno
Attorney General

Daniel Marcus
Acting Associate Attorney General

Mary Lou Leary
Acting Assistant Attorney General

Julie E. Samuels
Acting Director, National Institute of Justice

Office of Justice Programs
World Wide Web Site:
http://www.ojp.usdoj.gov

National Institute of Justice
World Wide Web Site:
http://www.ojp.usdoj.gov/nij

www.ingramcontent.com/pod-product-compliance
Lightning Source LLC
Chambersburg PA
CBHW080603180526
45168CB00007B/2758

9781514392355